wrap it up

D1122616

wrap it up

100 FRESH, BOLD, AND BRIGHT SANDWICHES WITH A TWIST

AMY COTLER

THREE RIVERS PRESS
NEW YORK

Copyright © 1998 by Amy Cotler

Published by Three Rivers Press, a division of Crown Publishers, Inc., 201 East 50th Street, New York, New York 10022. Member of the Crown Publishing Group.

Random House, Inc. New York, Toronto, London, Sydney, Auckland
www.randomhouse.com

THREE RIVERS PRESS and colophon are trademarks of Clarkson N. Potter, Inc.

Printed in the United States of America

Design by Maggie Hinders

Library of Congress Cataloging-in-Publication Data
Cotler, Amy.
    Wrap it up : 100 fresh, bold, and bright sandwiches with a twist /
by Amy Cotler. — 1st pbk. ed.
    Includes index.
    1. Sandwiches.   I. Title.
TX818.C584   1998
641.8'4—dc21   97–31689

ISBN 0-609-80236-4

10 9 8 7 6 5 4 3 2 1

First Paperback Edition

contents

For Aunt Ida

acknowledgments

Many thanks to Katie Workman, my talented editor, who brought out the best in this book; her dedicated assistant, Erica Youngren; my supportive agent, Jane Dystel; my assistant, Kate Baldwin, for her culinary fortitude and fun outlook; and, of course, to my family, Tommy and Emma, who enthusiastically ate hundreds of wraps.

introduction

It's a Wrap

Like most Americans, I long for fast, fresh, and fun ways to create food that's both healthy and delicious. Wraps—which encompass a wide variety of food enclosed in edible wrappers—fit the bill perfectly because they use readily available fresh foods, assembled with ease and imagination.

Wraps grew out of the American passion for burritos and international foods with plenty of flavor. They are distinctly American, bringing together our diverse culinary heritage, our thirst for bold flavors, and our irreverent but imaginative blending of foods, like adding Thai food to a tortilla or fresh mango salsa to a Texas barbecue.

My addiction to wraps started when I married my husband, Tom, in the early eighties. While I was preparing decadent catered meals for my clients in Manhattan, Tom, who grew up in Mexico, was throwing all the leftovers into tortillas. They tasted great—a gourmet's version of fast food, a new kind of sandwich, reborn burritos with international scope. By the time our daughter was in preschool, she was taking wraps, like the Reggae Roll, for lunches. Soon I got in the habit of keeping plenty of flatbreads on hand for last-minute meals—I was hooked. (In fact once my visiting mom, rummaging through my freezer for a meal, complained that all I stocked was tortillas.)

Now portable international wraps are sweeping the nation—and this is no fleeting trend; wraps are here to stay. The current popularity of international cuisines, especially Mediterranean, Asian, and Mexican, as well as the increasing accessibility of once-difficult-to-find ingredients, helps fuel this culinary innovation. Further, a burgeoning number of wrap restaurants, offering a wide variety of wraps, from made-on-the-spot tortillas with a choice of Latin fillings, to California-style wraps filled with an exciting array of international foods, have sparked America's interest in this versatile sandwich. Even more upscale restaurants are joining the fray, introducing sophisticated versions of wraps on their menus.

The availability of ready-made wrappers makes it easy for home cooks to create wraps in their own kitchens. And although you can wrap food in almost anything from banana leaves to puff pastry dough, for convenience all the "wrappers" in this book are made with fresh store-bought items that are widely available—

mostly tortillas, mountain bread, pitas, and lavash. Wrap fresh ingredients in these flatbreads and they become the new sandwich—international, economical, easily assembled, versatile, and fun to eat. Like the sandwich, they are portable, can be casual or fancy, and require little cooking technique. Their relaxed style liberates both the novice and the experienced cook. And these flexible recipes will inspire you to switch, swap, and substitute ingredients—to enjoy assembling an edible package of tasty foods.

Wrapping is part of an age-old tradition. We delight in bundles of goodies, wrapped up like surprise presents to enjoy. I hope this book embraces and goes beyond the current wrap movement, including and updating traditional food combinations and introducing fresh ideas, tasty meals, and loads of fun into your kitchen. I'll be there in spirit when you cut your first wrap open and witness the swirl of fresh colorful ingredients inside.

1 the wrap

A Cook's Guide

THE NATURE OF WRAPS

There was something inherently amusing about creating these wraps. My assistant, Kate, and I laughed a lot; the brief moment between completing and eating the wrap is titillating, full of expectation. Slicing them open to expose their savory (and gorgeous) fillings often brought shrieks of pleasure. We discovered along the way that wraps are playful, immediate, yet filled with possibilities. The nature of wraps is empowering. Even to the novice cook they're flexible and fun, with a big payback for little exertion. After trying a few recipes, and hopefully coming back for lots more, I hope you'll venture off on your own, combining leftovers, pantry items, and/or whatever is in season, then wrapping them up. I'd love to hear about your successes and failures, to share your surprises about what worked. Feel free to let me know at cotler@bcn.net.

SEALING AND STORAGE

Why seal a wrap? Although most wraps are thoroughly portable, some, especially salad wraps, hold together better when sealed in paper, plastic, or foil. Sealing also helps them keep better.

When storing a wrap, I seal it in wax paper; it is both aesthetically pleasing and ecological. (If you prefer, foil or plastic wrap works equally well.) First seal your wrap and then, if you desire, when you are ready to eat it, cut it in half on the bias.

To seal wraps you plan on reheating in the oven (see page 13), foil is best. For wraps you want to reheat in the microwave (see page 13), seal any way you prefer. Then, when you are ready to heat the wrap, unseal to prevent it from steaming too much.

You can cut assembly time if you lay your flatbread on top of wax paper or foil before you start wrapping. Then, for sealed wraps in one step, roll them up together, always being sure the paper doesn't get wrapped into the food.

How well do wraps keep? For the most part, unless the recipe says "eat immediately," wraps store wonderfully well, as well as, often better than, sandwiches. For transport and/or storage, it is essential to seal your wrap. For detailed information, see the Make Ahead/Take Away notes at the end of each recipe.

RECIPE NOTES

For your convenience, Substitutions, Short-cuts, Trim the Fat and Make Ahead/Take Away are included at the end of each recipe. Bear in mind that most if not all of the recipes are easily cut in half or doubled.

Substitutions

Look for substitutions in the ingredient list or below the recipe. Some of the suggestions I've made for ingredient substitutions, like using large burrito-size flour tortillas instead of lavash or chicken instead of turkey, are fairly straightforward. But wraps are very flexible, so if you can't find an item or just want to fool around with another ingredient, you'll usually meet with success—wraps enjoy experimentation.

Shortcuts

When creating these recipes, my aim was to get the best wraps possible in a minimum amount of time, so simple shortcuts are usually included within the recipes. But occasionally I suggest additional helpful shortcuts in the notes below the recipe.

Trim the Fat

Many of the wraps in this book are very low in fat. But some wraps, like some sandwiches, are not always inherently low in fat. (For a low-fat wraps list, see page 29.) In fact, take-out wraps are often quite high in fat. That's one of the great advantages of making your own—you can control the fat content.

If you want to improvise your own low-fat wraps, you should start out with ingredients that are relatively low in fat, including fish, vegetables, white-meat poultry, and lean cuts of red meat, like pork loin. Next, when cooking the fillings, use techniques that require little or no fat. For sautéing, nonstick pans are helpful tools, and lean cooking techniques like steaming and roasting (with ingredients tossed in little or no fat) as opposed to frying are good options.

When you are ready to assemble your own creation, be aware that wraps, like sandwiches, often require a moist spread between bread and filling. The challenge is to add moisture without fat. So when inventing your own wraps, try spreading the wrapper with convenient household staples. A few of my favorites are grainy or Dijon mustard; Major grey's chutney (or plain yogurt and chutney combined with a sprinkling of curry powder), yogurt mixed with other seasonings like harrissa or cayenne pepper, hoisin sauce, and plum sauce mixed with Dijon mustard. You may want to try low-fat mayonnaise or sour cream as well. A spread isn't essential if the filling is moist, so before wrapping try topping your filling with salsa or sliced or chopped tomatoes, or you can toss ingredients in a low-fat dressing or fresh lemon/lime juice or vinegar or even a bit of tomato sauce.

A final note: Wrappers are not high in fat, but low-fat tortillas are often available if you prefer.

Make Ahead/Take Away (and Reheating)

Recipes include notes on making wraps ahead as well as taking them along. Wraps can be taken along assembled, although a few recipes suggest packaging the contents and wrappers separately to prevent sogginess. Some wraps will not keep or transport well; in such cases, I have specified that they are best if eaten immediately.

One of the conveniences of do-ahead wraps is that they can be eaten in a variety of ways—cold, room temperature, or warm. When possible, for peak flavor, try to take chilled wraps out of the refrigerator 15 minutes or so before you eat them. Many of the warm wraps in this book can be eaten at room temperature, but they can also be reheated in the oven or microwave. The general rule is to heat them until just warmed all the way through. This will vary a little from wrap to wrap, so be attentive when reheating. Most wraps will reheat, wrapped in foil, in a preheated 350°F oven for about 10 to 15 minutes. The microwave is the most convenient way to heat wraps. Just take care not to overdo it, or they will become soggy. Unseal each wrap, place on a plate, and microwave as is or place in a shallow bowl, covered with a plate, and microwave for about 1 minute. The amount of time will vary greatly, depending on the power of your microwave.

STANDBYS—FLATBREAD, RICE, AND OTHER WRAP STAPLES

Flatbread

I keep a stash of one or more kinds of flatbread—tortillas, lavash, mountain bread, and pita—in my freezer. That way I can create wraps out of household staples and/or leftovers. Actually, sometimes they seem to dominate my freezer space, but that's worth sacrificing for the safety net they provide for emergency meals. Of course you can keep tortillas, lavash, mountain bread, and pita in the fridge as well, but, like all bread, they will turn stale quickly (especially pocket pitas and lavash), so keep an eye out. Flour tortillas seem to keep the longest.

Take frozen flatbreads out a little before you need them so you can pull them apart. If you don't have the time and they are stuck together, microwave them very briefly, just until you can separate them. Heat them as the recipe requires, and voilà, you're ready to wrap.

Rice

A fair number of the recipes in this book use rice, and if you have it on hand you can also create your own wraps in a few minutes. So when I cook rice I always make extra (it keeps well). You can even cook it and freeze it in a zippered plastic bag.

The easiest way to cook extra rice for wraps is to boil it like pasta. For 2 cups of rice, bring a 4-quart pot of salted water to a rapid boil. Add 1 cup of white or brown rice and boil until cooked through but still a tiny bit springy (you can pull a few grains out with a slotted spoon to taste), about 18 minutes for white and 35 minutes for brown. Drain well, then place under cold running water to stop the cooking, shake the colander to remove excess water, and store in a well-sealed container for up to 3 days. I like this technique because, unlike steamed rice, the grains always stay separate. Also, it's such a simple process that you can do plenty of other things while the rice cooks.

Household Staples

Having some of these items on hand helps out when you don't have time to shop.

Pantry

Beans, such as black, cannellini, pinto, kidney, and chickpeas (canned)

Broth, such as chicken and vegetable (canned or in bouillion cubes)

Bulgur wheat

Chilies, such as anchos (dried)

Chilies, such as chopped mild chilies and chipotle in adobo sauce (canned)

Coconut milk (canned)

Couscous

Fish, such as sardines, anchovies, tuna, salmon (canned)

Garlic

Herbs, such as thyme, oregano, basil, and rosemary (dried)

Hot sauce, such as Tabasco sauce

Mustard

Nuts

Oils, such as olive and canola

Onions

Peanut butter

Pickles

Potatoes

Rice

Soy Sauce

Spices, such as curry powder, cayenne pepper, cumin, and paprika

Stewed, whole, or diced tomatoes (canned)

Sun-dried tomatoes, in olive oil or packaged dry

Vinegars, such as red wine, cider, and balsamic

Worcestershire sauce

Refrigerated and Frozen

Anchovy paste

Black-eyed peas (frozen)

Capers

Cheese, such as Cheddar, Parmesan, Swiss, and goat cheese

Chutney

Eggs

Garlic

Greens, such as lettuce, cabbage, escarole, spinach, or kale

Hoisin sauce

Lemons and limes

Mayonnaise, reduced-fat and/or regular

Mustard, Dijon and grainy

Olives or olivada (an olive paste)

Onions

Pesto (refrigerated or frozen)

Pickled jalapeños

Salad dressings

Salsa

Sour cream, reduced fat and/or regular

Yogurt

SEASON TO TASTE: SALT, HERBS, AND SPICE

No doubt about it, salt brings out the flavor in food. But we all have a different palate for salt, so use recipes as a general guideline and salt to taste.

I hope you'll take lots of these wraps along for lunch. Cold mutes flavors, so, when you can, take them out of the fridge 15 minutes or more before eating them. When preparing a wrap that will be eaten completely cold, season more heavily than usual. If you are cutting down on salt, you can pump up the other herbs and spices in the wrap to fool your taste buds.

I leave the spiciness to you as well. Most of these wraps are spiced conservatively because I know I can count on you heat lovers to add more chilies, hot sauce, and freshly ground pepper to everything. Use the recipes only as a guide and season to suit your personal taste (see Some Like It Hot, page 30).

EQUIPMENT

You can prepare any of these wraps with common kitchen equipment, but certain inexpensive items are very helpful.

A nonstick skillet enables you to cook without a lot of fat and facilitates easy cleanup. A cast-iron or heavy skillet is helpful for toasting tortillas and mountain bread. A cast-iron ridged grill pan, although not essential, allows you to get some of that grilled flavor indoors, even in a small city kitchen. Cast-iron grill pans are inexpensive and turn out grilled food effortlessly. I even think they leave a slightly smoked taste on the food, which shouldn't be possible. My students tell me that they enjoy impressing friends when they leave restaurant-style seared grill marks on fish, vegetables, or meat. Grill pans are available in hardware and kitchen supply stores, in various sizes— small to fit a small kitchen or large enough to fit across two burners and grill for guests.

To seal wraps, keep foil around for wrapping pocketless pita bread and wraps that will be reheated in the oven and wax paper (or plastic if you prefer) for everything else. Finally, a pair of tongs makes turning tortillas over a gas flame or in a skillet effortless.

BUILDING YOUR OWN—THE FLAVOR PRINCIPLE

There are tips all over this book for creating your own wraps from seasonal foods, leftovers, or whatever strikes your wrap whim. But it is helpful to keep in mind that flavor is the key to inventing even the subtlest wrap. The filling needs plenty of flavor, more than the traditional bread-based sandwich, to hold up to the neutral wrapper. In fact, while developing these recipes I often found myself adding substantially more fresh lemon juice, spices, and other seasonings than I had initially thought necessary. So check Standbys—Flatbread, Rice, and Other Wrap Staples (page 13) for zingy ingredients to have on hand and the recipe chapter introductions for plenty of improvisational ideas.

THE NAMES ARE PICKED TO PROTECT THE INNOCENT— A NOTE ON AUTHENTICITY

True, there is an ancient tradition of wrapping food. No doubt some of these wraps are the great-great grandchildren of traditional wrapped foods. But for the most part they are an amalgam of cuisines, filling the need for quality fast-food that includes and combines a multitude of cultural flavors.

In the spirit of fun, the recipe names were picked to entice you, as well as suggest the flavors in the wrap, not to identify authentic regional dishes. So please don't go searching for the Madras Double-Mango Chicken in Madras, India!

Of course time doesn't stand still, and neither does authenticity. Contemporary American cuisine is evidence that "classic" dishes evolve, change. Perhaps fifty years from now our most popular wraps will be considered traditional late-twentieth-century American food!

Part of what makes this country's food so great (and sometimes so awful) is our ability to change, mix, and match. And because of our diverse society, we can enjoy Cuban, Thai, and Cajun cuisine, all in the same week (or even on the same plate!). The evolution of our polyglot society makes these wraps distinctly American and a lot of flavorful fun.

ACCOMPANIMENTS

What do you eat with a wrap? Many, if not most, of the wraps in this book stand on their own as ready-to-go one-dish meals.

If you want a side dish, many wraps can be accompanied by anything that you'd serve with a sandwich, like salads, soups, coleslaw, pickles, or potatoes in their many guises. But since wraps break the boundaries of sandwich making, so can sides; add to the plate whatever amuses you.

One gentle warning: Many wraps contain a lot more diverse ingredients than sandwiches, so when choosing an accompaniment, be careful not to repeat what's inside. (You don't need a green salad if your wrap is packed with greens.) Instead, choose accompaniments as you would for any kind of recipe, looking for foods that contrast nicely in terms of texture and flavor. Here are a few simple examples, just to get the ball rolling. . . .

For a wrap such as Santa Fe Chicken Wrap, try a few wedges of crunchy jícama (a sweet root vegetable) with a sprinkling of lime juice and cayenne pepper. Or, if it's winter, try a side of black beans. When greens aren't included in the wrap, especially for the Mediterranean-style wraps, a simple salad tossed with olive oil, vinegar, salt, and pepper can be a fine complement. For Asian wraps, try a coleslaw of shredded cabbage and fresh ginger tossed in a simple salad dressing, perhaps flavored with sesame oil.

Many wrap restaurants sell wraps with fruit smoothies. These are easily made with a blender, a few ice cubes, and plenty of fruit. They can include dairy, such as fresh or frozen yogurt or milk, or can be made using juice or sorbet. It is best to drink smoothies immediately after blending.

TAKE-OUT REVISITED

Take-out food has its place in this world, especially for busy weeknights. After all, wraps made their debut as a quick fix/take-out item. But when you have a few minutes, the advantages of assembling your own wraps are enormous.

Wrap it up yourself to season to your own taste, like adding lots of garlic and spices or tailoring a wrap to a kid's plain palate; eliminate or reduce fat or salt; make substitutions, such as chicken thighs for breasts, shrimp for crab; cook fillings to the desired doneness; eliminate cheap fillers; and shop for what's fresh and seasonal.

The potential for variety is virtually endless; the hundred wraps here with variations are just the tip of the iceberg. Your own wraps will run circles around the ten to twenty pickings at your local wrapperama. If you're in a hurry and you want to avoid that take-out temptation, check out 20-Minutes-and-Under Wraps (page 28).

2 wrapper road map

A Wrapper Reference Trip Around the World

TORTILLAS

A Mexican tortilla is a thin round flat-bread, made with unleavened wheat flour or cornmeal dough. Although corn tortillas dominate all but northern Mexico, wraps, for the most part, use large burrito-size flour tortillas, because they roll beautifully into self-contained portable sandwiches.

Tortillas have always been popular in the Southwest, but over the last decade they have been assimilated into American culture everywhere. No wonder, from my intensive recipe testing, I've dubbed them "the universal wrap." They are so flexible: Almost anything goes well inside a tortilla, and once heated briefly to make them pliable they can be used in a multitude of wrapping techniques.

Style and Size
Style
White flour

Size
Large (burrito size)—about 9-inch
  diameter
small (fajita and taco size)—about 6½ to
  8-inch diameter

Depending on the brand, fajita size is generally a little smaller. Use the size called for in the recipes; otherwise they are close enough in size to be used interchangeably.

Style
Corn

Size
One size—about 6-inch diameter
"taco" shell (hard)

Other Styles
Uncommon tortillas—blue corn,
  sprouted or whole wheat, chipotle
  pepper, tomato, and spinach

Where to Find
In the supermarket: Fresh tortillas are available in the refrigerated dairy section; taco shells are found in the Latin or Hispanic section. More unusual styles can also be found at health food or specialty food stores. Compare brands since the quality varies, especially with corn. Sometimes, in locations where there is a large Mexican population, you can purchase freshly made tortillas from a tortilla factory or a Mexican restaurant.

How to Store

Store in the refrigerator. You can also store tortillas in the freezer. Defrost in the refrigerator, or, if they are not stuck together, they can be heated directly from frozen. If you are in a hurry and frozen tortillas are stuck together, heat them in the microwave briefly, just until they can be pulled apart.

How to Heat

Why heat a tortilla? Although some feel it isn't essential to heat a tortilla, I much prefer heating them, even if they are later eaten cold, because they tend to have a better flavor and texture and are far more rollable. As with all flatbreads, the key is to heat them until warm and pliable but not brittle, so less is better than more. Luckily, the durable tortilla takes to a wide variety of heating methods.

Tortilla Heating Techniques

Hands down, my favorite technique for heating flour tortillas is right over a grill or an open gas flame. It is lightning-quick, easy, and imparts a toasted flavor to the tortillas. For those with an electric stove, a close second is on a heavy skillet. These techniques are listed with most of the tortilla wraps in this book. But for the purposes of both convenience and flexibility, I have listed here a wide variety of alternative heating techniques.

Flour Tortillas

Gas Flame, Open Fire, Skillet

For flour tortillas: Using tongs, place the tortillas, one at a time, directly onto a medium-high gas flame or grill rack, turning every couple of seconds until hot and pliable, for a total of about 5 to 7 seconds each. Or use a large skillet, preferably heavy or cast-iron, first heating it until hot, then adding the tortillas, one a time, to the dry skillet until they start to buckle on one side. Turn them and heat the second side, about 10 to 15 seconds on each side. Use immediately or, to hold, stack them together and wrap in a large kitchen towel.

Microwave Steamed

The microwave is a quick, convenient way to steam-soften tortillas, because they can be done all at once. Stack the number of tortillas called for in the recipe between two damp microwave-proof paper towels and microwave until hot and pliable, about 10 seconds per tortilla. Timing will depend on the power of your microwave, so keep a sharp lookout the first time, and then you will have the timing down. (Note that some tortilla brands are naturally much wetter than others, so they do not require damp paper towels.) Keep the tortillas covered as you are assembling the wraps.

Stove Top Steamed

Although less convenient, tortillas hold longer when steamed on top of the stove.

Wrap your tortillas in a heavy kitchen towel and set in a steamer over ½ inch of boiling water. Cover. Steam for 1 minute, then turn off the heat and let stand for 10 to 15 minutes. The steamer can even be placed in a 200°F oven for up to an hour. Add a few extra tortillas to the stack since the top and bottom ones may fall apart.

Oven

If you are already using the oven to cook your wrap contents, it can be practical to heat your tortillas in there as well. Simply wrap with foil and heat in a preheated oven until warm and pliable, about 2 to 10 minutes, depending on how many tortillas you are heating and your oven (just make sure they are warm but not brittle).

To Hold Once They Are Warm

For most of these recipes the tortillas are heated and then immediately filled. But you may prefer to put out the ingredients and let diners roll their own. Once tortillas have been warmed using any of the listed techniques, they can be stored, wrapped tightly in foil, in a 200°F oven for up to 1 hour. Or store warm tortillas traditionally, wrapped in a cloth inside a basket, for about half an hour.

Corn Tortillas

Most packaged corn tortillas in this country tend to be dry. So use a skillet instead of the direct-heat gas flame or grill techniques described earlier. Just wet your hands and rub them across the tortillas.

Heat a heavy, preferably cast-iron, skillet over medium heat. Add up to 4 tortillas at a time, stacking them together in the skillet. Heat so they steam soft, rotating them every few seconds with tongs, until hot and pliable, about 1 to 2 minutes.

If you are lucky enough to be able to purchase soft, pliable corn tortillas from a tortilla factory or Mexican restaurant, they can be heated using any of the same techniques as for flour tortillas. Heating them is preferable—using a skillet, grill, or gas flame—because this brings out the corn flavor.

Reheating Tortilla Wraps

Many of these wraps are good at room temperature or even cold, but many benefit from a brief reheating as well. Wrap in foil and heat, just until warm, 10 to 15 minutes in a preheated 350°F oven. Or heat on a plate in the microwave, uncovered, until just warm, about 1 minute. Better to underheat rather than overheat any wrap in the microwave, because it can get soggy.

Wrapping with Tortillas

Wrapping is described in specific recipes, most of which use large burrito-size tortillas. Unless instructed otherwise, the ingredients should be distributed horizontally in a thick strip across the bottom third of the tortilla, so that the ingredients don't quite touch the sides. Then, to prevent dripping, usually both (sometimes one) sides are folded in, and then you roll the wrap up and away from you. (To form a tighter, more compact wrap, first fold the side facing you over the filling, then fold the sides in before you roll it up.) Occasionally, the recipe instructs you to scatter the filling evenly over the tortilla and then roll it up. This incorporates the bread and filling, creating a spiral when the bread is cut in half. In this case, if you wish, the ends may be cut off.

For presentation, sometimes the instructions direct you to fold in only one side before rolling, leaving the other side open to display the contents. Or, I like to fold in both sides and cut wraps in half on the bias, because the colorful filling is tempting, and, as with sandwiches, halves are easier to handle. If serving on a plate, one half can be propped up by the other so that they overlap. (Hot wraps with juicy contents should remain whole.)

A note on heating tortillas so that they wrap easily: Heating tortillas is a snap (see page 19). Just bear in mind that for wrapping the key is not to overcook the tortilla. If you heat it in the skillet or on a gas flame or grill, it takes a very short time; the tortilla should still be quite pliable, not crisp. Alternatively, if you steam it, it should be soft but not mushy; otherwise it will fall apart.

Wrap Swap
A lavash rectangle takes about the same amount of ingredients as a large burrito-size tortilla, so feel free to substitute one for the other.

PITAS
The pita is a traditional bread found all over the eastern Mediterranean. There are two kinds of pita commonly available. The first has a pocket, which is created when the dough puffs during baking, then deflates, leaving a hollow in the middle. Pocket pitas can be cut open and stuffed with a multitude of ingredients or split apart, topped, and rolled. Thicker, pocketless pitas are also widely available. Once heated, I find pocketless pitas extremely versatile and especially satisfying for those who crave a bread texture in their wraps.

Style and Size
Style
White and whole wheat

Size
Pocket Pita: standard (5–6 inches), sandwich (about 4 inches), mini (2–3 inches)
Pocketless (about 6 inches)

Recipes that call for pocketless pita were tested with unseasoned pitas, since they are more commonly available. But where appropriate, feel free to substitute pitas seasoned with garlic or onions, for example.

Where to Find
Pitas are found in the deli or bread section of your supermarket. Look carefully at expiration dates; pita bread tends to dry out quickly.

How to Store

Pita pockets, both with and without pockets, should be stored in the refrigerator. Both can be frozen and should be defrosted in the refrigerator. Pitas can be defrosted in the microwave very briefly, just until soft but not mushy, then heated according to recipe instructions.

How to Heat

It is not essential to heat pocket pitas. Pocketless pitas should be heated, however, since it enhances their texture radically. Wraps should be assembled while the pita is still warm and pliable.

Broiler

Unless you are already using the oven, or your broiler takes forever to preheat, broiling is the simplest way to heat pocketless pitas. Brush one side with oil and broil until very slightly crisp but not brittle (or they will not roll well), about 1 minute. Place the ingredients on the softer (unbroiled) side before wrapping.

Oven

When your filling is cooked in the oven, it is convenient to heat your pocketless pitas there as well. Heat them dry or with one side lightly brushed with olive oil, directly on the racks of a preheated 350°F to 425°F oven, for 2 to 5 minutes, until hot but still pliable.

Stove Top/Skillet

One at a time, pocketless pitas may be heated dry or with one side lightly brushed with oil, in a hot, dry heavy skillet, preferably cast-iron, until hot and pliable but not brittle, about 30 seconds to 1 minute on each side.

Reheating Pocketless Pita Wraps

While many of these wraps are great at room temperature, you can also wrap them in foil and heat in the oven until hot, about 15 minutes at 350°F. Some wraps have liquidy contents that can soak the pita (some people enjoy that, while others do not). With few exceptions, when preparing the filling beforehand, I prefer to reheat it, then fold it into a freshly heated pita just before eating.

"Wrapping" with Pitas

Pita Pocket

Cut a strip from the top that is large enough to allow the ingredients easy access into the pocket. Or, to reduce the size of your sandwich, a pita may be cut in half. In a few of the recipes the pita is cut open horizontally, leaving two rounds. Each round is topped and cooked, then rolled. Use a paring knife to split the pita. This takes a little practice, so have a few extra pitas on hand for backup.

Pocketless Pita

Lay warm pita (see above), cooked side down, on a 12-inch sheet of foil, with the top of the bread placed 2 to 3 inches above the edge of the foil. Place the filling in a strip up the middle, leaving attractive items like arugula leaves or tomato wedges at the top for a savory presentation. Wrap the warm pita, side to side, into a cone, wrapping the bread and the foil so it serves as a support and seals the bottom to prevent dripping. Alternatively, especially when grilling, it is fun to use the pocket pita like focaccia. Lay it flat on a plate, top decoratively with the ingredients, and let the diners rip and roll their own.

Wrap Swap

Pocket and pocketless pitas are widely available. In some areas you can find naan, Indian flatbread, which is sometimes sold in a variety of flavors. It can be used to replace pocketless pita.

LAVASH

Lavash is another ancient flatbread, originally from Armenia. Name Jeffrey Alford and Naomi Duguid, authors of *Flatbreads and Flavors*, describe going to an Armenian market and buying lavash by the kilo that measured four by five feet! Here the most commonly available lavash is far smaller but still extremely versatile (and a lot of fun) to use.

Lavash has a distinct advantage over most commercial flatbreads; it isn't essential to heat it to make it pliable enough to roll. It is a delicate bread with a lovely, naturally uneven texture. Lavash usually comes in rectangles, which lends them to a stunning presentation when rolled into logs and cut on the bias into two or more pieces.

Style and Size

Style

White flour (Whole wheat lavash is less frequently available)

Size

About 8½ by 10 inches

Recipes were tested with the most commonly available lavash, but other sizes are available. Lavash may be cut "standard" size, or recipes can be adapted to another size.

Where to Find

Lavash is often in the deli section of supermarkets, near the pita and mountain bread. It is not always easy to find, but as wraps get more popular availability is increasing.

How to Store

Because it is not always available, when I find lavash I buy several packages and freeze them. They keep well in the refrigerator, but not for long, since they tend to dry out. So if you are not going to use it all within a day or two, freeze it. Defrost it in the refrigerator or at room temperature. If it does get dry, heat it for 5 to 10 seconds in the microwave to make it more pliable.

Wrapping with Lavash

The most commonly available lavash is roughly a 9- by 10-inch rectangle. Unless otherwise stated, it can be rolled from either edge. But be sure to check specific recipe directions, which sometimes call for rolling from the short end to help hold the wrap together.

There are two ways to distribute fillings on lavash bread. The first technique is to lay the filling in a thick horizontal strip, a third of the way up from the bottom, then roll it up away from you. The second is to sprinkle the ingredients all over the bread, then roll as tightly as possible without tearing. This technique will create a dramatic spiral, but it doesn't hold together for all kinds of wraps. With fluffy fillings, like salad, you will have to compress the filling as you roll, pulling the lavash under and a little toward you as you wrap. Served as is, or rolled in wax paper and cut in the center on the bias, lavash makes a smashing wrap. Watch that the paper doesn't get rolled into the wrap.

Wrap Swap

If you find lavash in larger pieces, cut it to the roughly 9- by 10-inch rectangles called for in the recipe or add more filling. Finally, don't despair if you can't find lavash at all, since you can easily replace it with a heated large burrito-size flour tortilla, which takes the same amount of filling.

MOUNTAIN BREAD

In many Middle Eastern countries, like Iran and Lebanon, flatbread is thought of as mountain bread because it is the staple bread of the mountain peoples. A variation of mountain bread is now available in most supermarkets.

It is easy to describe mountain bread by comparing it to the flatbread most Americans are familiar with—large burrito-size flour tortillas. Mountain bread is slightly thicker, so it is not quite as pliable. It is a little smaller and has a more breadlike texture than tortillas. Use mountain bread when you want a slightly more assertive texture and flavor. Whole-wheat mountain bread has a pronounced whole-wheat taste that goes well with robust fillings that complement this hearty bread. It also heats superbly in the oven, forming a crusty container for a moist filling, as in the Crispy Twice-Baked Bean and Cheese Wrap (page 95).

Style and Size
Style
White or whole-wheat flour

Size
About 7- to 8-inch diameter

Where to Find
Most commonly found in front of the deli or in the bakery section of most super-

markets, near the pita bread. Health food stores often sell mountain bread as well.

How to Store

Store mountain bread in the refrigerator. Check the expiration date to make sure it's fresh. Generally it will last for five days unopened and for three once opened.

How to Heat

Like most flatbread, mountain bread needs to be heated to make it pliable. Heating also makes its texture and taste more appealing. Mountain bread can be heated any way tortillas are heated, but it is best heated in a hot, dry skillet or wrapped in foil in the oven. (See Tortillas, page 19.)

Reheating Mountain Bread Wraps

Reheat mountain bread wraps as you would tortilla wraps (page 20).

Wrapping with Mountain Bread

As with tortillas, you don't want to start with a brittle bread, so cook just until pliable. Because it is thicker and breadier than tortillas, not all of the mountain bread wraps are folded in on the sides before they are rolled up. Just follow each recipe's directions. Like lavash and tortilla wraps, mountain bread can be cut in half on the bias for a pretty presentation.

Wrap Swap

If you prefer a more breadlike texture or simply like a whole-wheat flavor, use mountain bread in place of small tortillas. If you want to swap mountain bread for recipes that call for large burrito-size flour tortillas, the recipe will yield more wraps, because mountain bread will hold half to three quarters of the filling in each wrap. So a recipe for four wraps that calls for large burrito-size flour tortillas will make six to eight mountain bread wraps. If you prefer, taco-size flour tortillas can replace mountain bread.

OTHER WRAPPERS

More Unusual Flatbread Wrappers

In the spirit of convenience, the majority of the wraps in this book use easily accessible wrappers that can be purchased in a supermarket—mostly tortillas, pita, mountain bread, and lavash. But in large cities or areas where immigrant populations utilize other kinds of flatbreads—for example, Indian breads, like chapati and naan—a wider variety of wrappers may be available. Also, health food stores sometimes stock a wider variety of flatbreads. So, if you find a flatbread that inspires you, feel free to improvise, substituting one wrap of the approximate size and thickness for another.

Nonflatbread Wrappers

To celebrate the wrap as a flexible variation on the portable sandwich, and in line with the current wrap craze, wraps in this book use primarily flatbread wrappers. But if you are on a diet or looking for a lighter wrap, where appropriate, feel free to eliminate the bread entirely and use large lettuce leaves, or even try large cabbage leaves that are steamed briefly until wilted, then plunged into cold water and dried. Rice paper, which is tricky to find, is used in only two recipes in this book, where you will find complete directions for reconstituting and wrapping. Nori, a seaweed commonly used in sushi, can be found in health food and Asian specialty stores. It can be filled with the traditional sticky rice and seafood and/or cucumber with a touch of wasabi or even pickled ginger. Or invent your own hand roll using whatever is around.

3 wrapper roundup

A Quick Wrap Cross-reference

VEGETARIAN

A big chunk of *Wrap It Up* is vegetarian, not only because many people see wraps as a healthy alternative to fast food but also because vegetables taste great in wraps. Of course many of the recipes that don't qualify as vegetarian feature vegetables and greens, using meat, chicken, or fish as an accent. The entire Vegetable Wraps chapter is vegetarian, and so are the wraps in Bean and Legume Wraps, except Mess o' Greens and Beans.

*Those with eggs

Antipasto Wrap (page 63)

Blueberry Nectarine Blintz (page 192)

Camembert and Apple Chutney Crisp (page 193)

Cheese-in-a-Snap Wrap (page 194)

Chili Bean Wrap (page 92)

Corny Avocado Taco (page 61)

Crisp Broccoli Rabe "Manicotti" (page 62)

Crispy Twice-Baked Bean and Cheese Wrap (page 95)

Curried Couscous with Spinach and Chickpeas (page 98)

Egg Salad Rémoulade* (page 198)

Good to Eat Beet, Hazelnut, and Gorgonzola Wrap (page 64)

Hearty Veggie-Pesto Spiral (made with vegetable broth) (page 66)

Italian White Bean Burrito with Salsa Cruda (page 87)

It's Greek to Me Wrap (page 42)

Mediterranean Wrap (page 96)

Miami Beach Black Bean Wrap (page 94)

Minted Couscous Tabbouleh Roll (page 40)

Moroccan Cracked Wheat and Chickpea Roll-Up (page 100)

Panzanella (page 42)

Quick Chèvre Salad Wrap (page 197)

Reggae Roll (page 103)

Roasted Garlic Summer Roll (page 68)

Seventies Roll (page 70)

Smoky Eggplant Gyro (page 71)

Steamed Vegetable Wrap Two Ways (page 72)

Sweet Potato and Shiitake Mushroom Roll (page 78)

Taos Breakfast Roll with Ancho Chili Ketchup* (page 202)

Thai Noodle Veggie Wrap (page 82)

20-MINUTES-AND-UNDER WRAPS

Even a quick glance through this book will tell you that, with few exceptions, the emphasis is on lots of flavor in little time. These are the quickest of the bunch, but very few recipes in the entire book take more than 30 minutes.

LOW-FAT WRAPS

As a chef, teacher, and food writer, I have done a lot of work developing tasty, low-fat recipes, designing spa technique classes for Peter Kump's cooking school in Manhattan and working as a spa executive dining room chef. My philosophy is that flavor is most important, so I can guarantee that the low-fat recipes listed here taste great. In general, I like to avoid low-fat products, with the occasional exception of nonfat yogurt or low-fat cottage cheese. Rather, I reduce the fat in other ways, as you will see in the recipes. Of course, every one's palate is different, so if you like, reduce the fat further, by using other low-fat products, such as cheese or sour cream.

Take note that tortilla nutritional counts vary greatly, and fat may be reduced further by using nonfat tortillas. When using pocketless pita, omit the step where you brush with oil.

In accordance with current nutritional guidelines, the recipes listed here all have 30 percent or fewer calories deriving from fat (some have no added fat at all). Bear in mind that there are many other low-calorie wraps in *Wrap It Up*, especially in the Chapter 4 (salads) and Chapter 8 (fish and seafood). Some of the wraps are so low in calories that the small amount of fat still puts the total calories from fat at above 30 percent. Nevertheless, there are not many grams of fat in these recipes, so these wraps can easily be part of a healthful diet.

Also, remember that an alternative way to cut down on fat is to cut down on portions. For most of the recipes I have called for one wrap per person, but some of the wraps are quite hearty, so you can cut the recipe in half, and you'll reduce the fat by half!

**Low in fat when Trim the Fat directions at the end of the recipe are followed

Athenian Lamb Gyro with Tzatziki** (page 186)
California Wrap and Roll** (page 136)
Cheese-in-a-Snap Wrap** (page 194)
Chili Bean Wrap** (page 92)
Crispy Twice-Baked Bean and Cheese Wrap** (page 95)
Cuban Chicken, Rice, and Beans** (page 112)
Curried Couscous with Spinach and Chickpeas (page 98)
Diner Wrap** (page 178)
Garlic Chicken with Italian Green Sauce** (page 126)
Good to Eat Beet, Hazelnut, and Gorgonzola Wrap** (page 64)
Grilled Swordfish Salad** (page 52)
Italian White Bean Burrito with Salsa Cruda** (page 87)
Jambalaya Wrap (page 142)
Madras Double-Mango Chicken (page 114)
Mandarin Chicken Salad with Radicchio** (page 48)
Mediterranean Wrap** (page 96)
Mess o' Greens and Beans** (page 104)

SOME LIKE IT HOT

The wraps listed here take naturally to lots of spice. Generally all the recipes in this book call for the conservative use of hot spices, so season to taste.

NO-COOK WRAPS

Of course, many of the wraps involve very little cooking to start with, but these fillings aren't cooked at all!

BY CUISINE

Do you have a wrap whim for a specific kind of food? With wraps, creativity and flavor dominate authenticity, allowing you to be an armchair traveler as well as satisfying your cravings for a wide variety of foods, including Mediterranean, Asian, South (or just North) of the Border, or old-fashioned American home-cooking. But remember, there are plenty of wraps that don't fall neatly into these categories and could be categorized as fusion food, so as you flip through the pages, you'll find other ethnic offerings.

Asian

Latin, South (and Just North) of the Border

(Of course anything wrapped in a tortilla might be considered South of the Border!)

HORS D'OEUVRES

Cut these into small pieces and they make ideal appetizers. These are just some of the most appetizer-like recipes, but lots of other recipes lend themselves to serving one- or two-bite-size slices.

4 salad wraps

Toss 'n' Wrap

I'm a salad lover; but surprisingly, I often preferred these wraps to the many colorful salads that normally grace my table. Maybe this is because wrapped salads are so much fun to eat. Maybe it's biting through a mild chewy wrapper to a tangy salad below that's so eminently appealing. Or perhaps it's their novelty or portability. Now I can eat a tantalizing salad anywhere at all, like on a hike, in my car, or even while pacing on the phone! Best of all, now you can easily take a satisfying salad to work.

Ever eaten an hour-old wilted salad? Good news: Once wrapped, salads last longer. The wrapper seems to protect them a bit, and even if they deflate a little, they're still delicious—in fact, sometimes even better!

So now that I've sung the praises of the salad wrap, here's the lowdown: Salad wraps can be prepared 3 or 4 hours ahead, especially when you use crispy lettuce, like romaine. Or, if you prefer, you can get many of these recipes ready with the dressing on the side, toss them at the last minute, then wrap them up.

Be aware that, because of their nature, salad wraps can be crumbly. I like to wrap them in wax paper (or you can use plastic or foil) and cut them in half on the bias. The insides are pretty to look at, and then I fold down the paper on each half as I eat. Or as with the traditional burrito, you can eat them out of hand and then, if need be, finish with a fork.

You can easily create your own salad wraps with what's around. Bear in mind that you need a very flavorful dressing to hold up to the neutral wrap, often with more acid—vinegar or citrus juice—than you might like in an unwrapped salad. In a rush? Toss a salad bar salad, then wrap it up, as is, or add store-bought or leftover chicken, fish, meat, vegetables, or even hard-cooked eggs. Or make your own salad and salad dressing (or use bottled), then goose them up with extra vinegar, lemon juice, salsa, pickled jalapeños, or whatever you have on hand. (But don't dress the salad very heavily or the wrapper will get soggy.) As with all wraps, lots of flavor is the key, so add olives, feta, or whatever you have around with lots of punch. And if you eat them ice-cold, right out of the refrigerator, you might want to add a touch more salt before you roll, because cold dulls flavor (see page 15).

Finally, cut the components of your filling into small pieces; if they're too large, they may poke through and make holes in the wrapper.

Salad wraps are available here and there, but nothing beats the staggering variety of the seventeen salad wraps in this chapter, made with fresh ingredients you pick out yourself. So on to vibrant wraps like crunchy Coconut Curry Shrimp Salad, and Mandarin Chicken Salad with Radicchio, or juicy tomato Panzanella, perfumed with garlic and basil.

SALAD

Cobb Roll

Spinach Salad Wrap with Wild Mushrooms

Wild and Nutty Cups

Minted Couscous Tabbouleh Roll

It's Greek to Me Wrap

Panzanella

Et Tu Brute Roll

Steak Salad with Chimichurri Sauce

Vietnamese Pork and Lettuce Rolls

Mandarin Chicken Salad with Radicchio

Fall Salad Wrap

Sardinian Roll

Grilled Swordfish Salad

Riviera Roll

Coconut Curry Shrimp Salad

Shrimp Cucumber Sambal

Smoked Trout–Avocado Salad Cups

Cobb Roll

 The cobb salad, most likely invented as a way to use leftovers, was created at the Brown Derby restaurant in the 1920s. Since then, it has gone in and out of fashion, but it's a delicious salad and makes a luxurious wrap that holds well. This chopped salad wrap holds together best when sealed in foil.

4 strips of thick-cut slab bacon or any thick-cut bacon
2 boneless, skinless chicken breast halves, each cut in half
2 teaspoons red wine vinegar
2 teaspoons fresh lemon juice
2 teaspoons Dijon mustard
generous pinch of salt and freshly ground pepper
4 teaspoons olive oil
1 small head of iceberg lettuce, finely chopped
4 lavash rectangles
1 ripe small avocado, peeled, pitted, and diced
2 plum tomatoes, chopped
2 hard-cooked eggs, peeled and chopped, optional
⅓ cup crumbled blue cheese

1. Preheat the oven to 425°F. Roast the bacon and chicken together on a baking sheet, turning once with tongs, just until both are cooked through, about 10 to 12 minutes. When they are cool enough to handle, chop coarsely.

2. Meanwhile, mix together the vinegar, lemon juice, mustard, salt, and pepper in a large bowl. Slowly whisk in the oil. Toss the lettuce in the dressing.

3. To assemble: Place a lavash on a large piece of wax paper or foil. (This is a crumbly filling, so the wrap holds better that way.) With a short end facing you, pile about a quarter of the salad in a thick strip across the lavash, about a third of the way up from the bottom. Sprinkle about a quarter of the avocado, tomato, egg, blue cheese, chopped chicken, and bacon over the salad. Roll it up, curling the bread under with your fingers as you roll and being careful not to wrap the wax paper or foil into the spiral. Seal the ends. Complete the wraps with the remaining ingredients. Or, if you prefer, prepare all at once, assembly-line style. Cut in half on the bias. Peel down the foil as you eat.

MAKES 4 WRAPS

Substitutions

Large burrito-size tortillas may be substituted for the lavash. Try a wide variety of household leftovers in this wrap, like cooked chicken or turkey, or chopped cooked or raw vegetables.

Trim the Fat
To reduce the fat, replace the bacon with turkey bacon, cut the amount of cheese in half, and eliminate the avocado. You may also reduce the amount of oil in the dressing.

Make Ahead/Take Away
Sealed in wax paper, plastic wrap, or foil and refrigerated, the wraps keep for up to 4 hours before serving. Alternatively, the filling and dressing can be made the day before, then held separately in the refrigerator. Toss together and assemble as described before eating. Serve at room temperature or cold.

Spinach Salad Wrap
with Wild Mushrooms

 If you like classic spinach salads, you'll adore this update with roasted shiitakes and curry dressing.

8 strips of bacon
20 medium-size shiitake mushrooms, stems removed
2 medium onions, sliced
2 tablespoons cider vinegar
2 teaspoons curry powder
generous pinch of salt
1 10-ounce package washed spinach, stems removed
4 large burrito-size flour tortillas

1. Preheat the oven to 400°F. Lay the bacon on a baking sheet with the shiitake caps and onions on top. Roast for 5 minutes, then toss with tongs. Continue roasting until the bacon and mushrooms are cooked, another 5 to 7 minutes. Remove from the oven, leaving the oven on.

2. Meanwhile, whisk together the vinegar, curry, and salt in a large bowl.

3. Using tongs, remove the bacon, mushrooms, and onions from the baking sheet. Add them to the curry mixture with the spinach and toss well.

4. To assemble: Stack the tortillas, wrap in foil, and heat in the oven until warm, about 5 minutes. Or heat the tortillas, one at a time, directly on a gas flame, on a grill, or in a hot skillet, turning frequently, until hot and pliable, 5 to 15 seconds each. Alternatively, heat, stacked, in the microwave (see page 19). Lay a tortilla on top of a 12-inch square of foil. Place a quarter of the salad in a thick horizontal strip across the bottom third of a tortilla, making sure the ingredients don't quite touch the edges. Fold in the two sides and roll the wrap away from you, compressing the salad as you roll, being careful not to roll the foil into the spiral. Complete the wraps with the remaining ingredients. Or, if you prefer, prepare all at once, assembly-line style. Cut in half on the bias.

MAKES 4 WRAPS

Make Ahead/Take Away
Sealed in wax paper, foil, or plastic wrap and refrigerated, these wraps keep well for up to 3 hours before serving. Serve warm, at room temperature, or cold.

Wild and Nutty Cups

 More a cup than a wrap, this whole-grain salad, perfumed with toasted walnuts, makes a fine light lunch, casual knife-and-fork first course, or side dish with roasted chicken.

1 cup wild and brown rice blend
2 tablespoons vegetable oil
⅔ cup coarsely chopped walnuts
2 teaspoons cider vinegar
¼ teaspoon salt and freshly ground pepper or to taste
1 cup halved red grapes
2 small scallions, both white and green parts, trimmed and thinly sliced
4 large cup-shaped Boston lettuce leaves

1. Bring 2 quarts of generously salted water to a rapid boil. Add the rice and boil until tender but still a little firm, about 45 minutes. Drain and rinse with cold water.

2. Heat 1 tablespoon of the oil in a skillet. Add the nuts and cook over medium heat, stirring constantly, until toasted and aromatic, watching closely to avoid burning, 2 to 4 minutes. Add to a large bowl with the rice, remaining 1 tablespoon oil, vinegar, salt, and pepper. Toss well. Stir in the grapes and scallions.

3. To assemble: Spoon the salad into lettuce cups and serve. The sides may be folded in to eat by hand.

MAKES 4 WRAPS OR 8 SMALL SIDE-DISH WRAPS IN SMALLER LETTUCE CUPS.

Substitutions
You can buy a blend of brown and wild rice in a bag at the supermarket, mix your own, or buy any rice blend and cook, without the seasoning package, according to the box directions.

Trim the Fat
To reduce the fat, cut the oil in half and replace with chicken stock.

Make Ahead/Take Away
Leave out at room temperature for up to 3 hours until ready to eat, stirring in the nuts before assembling and serving. Serve at room temperature.

Minted Couscous
Tabbouleh Roll

 A refreshing summer roll that is excellent either at room temperature or icy cold. Tabbouleh is usually made with bulgur wheat, but here I've added the traditional seasonings of garlic, lemon juice, and fresh herbs to light and fluffy couscous.

¾ cup plain couscous
½ teaspoon salt, plus more if needed
1 garlic clove, peeled
2 tablespoons fresh lemon juice
2 tablespoons olive oil, preferably extra-virgin
¼ cup packed fresh parsley leaves
scant ¼ cup packed fresh mint leaves
2 scallions, both white and green part, trimmed and cut into thirds
freshly ground pepper to taste
4 large burrito-size flour tortillas
12 to 16 green leaf or romaine lettuce leaves
1 large ripe tomato, cut in half and sliced
1 small Kirby cucumber, cut in half lengthwise and sliced

1. Place the couscous and ½ teaspoon salt in large heatproof mixing bowl, then pour in 1 cup boiling water. Cover tightly and let sit for 5 minutes.

2. Meanwhile, make the dressing. With the motor running, drop the garlic and lemon juice into a food processor, then drizzle in the olive oil. Stop the machine and add the parsley, mint, and scallions, pulsing several times to chop roughly. Stir the dressing into the couscous and season with salt and pepper. (If you plan on chilling the roll, salt it more heavily

than if you will be eating it at room temperature.)

3. To assemble: Heat the tortillas, one at a time, directly on a gas flame, on a grill, or in a hot skillet, turning frequently, until hot and pliable, 5 to 15 seconds each. Or heat, stacked, in the microwave (see page 19). Lay down 3 to 4 lettuce leaves, topped with ¼ of the couscous salad, and ¼ of the tomatoes and cucumber in a thick horizontal strip across the bottom third of the tortilla, making sure the ingredients don't quite touch the

edges. Fold in the two sides and roll the wrap away from you. Complete the wraps with the remaining ingredients. Or, if you prefer, prepare all at once, assembly-line style. Cut in half on the bias.
MAKES 4 WRAPS

Substitutions
This makes a great lettuce wrap. Just skip the tortilla and use large leaves of green leaf lettuce instead.

Trim the Fat
This is a low-fat wrap if the oil is cut by 1 teaspoon.

Make Ahead/Take Away
Sealed in wax paper, foil, or plastic wrap and refrigerated, the wraps keep well for up to 6 hours. Serve at room temperature or cold.

It's Greek to Me Wrap

 Forget about the been-there-done-that Greek salads and bite into this lemony, minty wrap.

1 tablespoon fresh lemon juice
2 tablespoons coarsely grated Parmesan cheese
2 teaspoons chopped fresh mint leaves
1 large garlic clove, finely minced
2 tablespoons olive oil, preferably fruity
1 large or 2 small Kirby cucumbers, diced
1 large ripe tomato, coarsely chopped
½ cup coarsely chopped Vidalia onion or ¼ cup chopped red onion
10 Kalamata or 8 oil-cured black olives, halved and pitted
2 cups shredded romaine lettuce, preferably hearts
⅓ cup crumbled feta cheese
salt and freshly ground pepper to taste
2 lavash rectangles

1. Place the lemon juice, Parmesan, mint, and garlic in a large bowl. With a fork, mix in the olive oil. Add the cucumber, tomato, onion, and olives and toss. Toss again with the romaine and feta, adding salt and pepper if necessary.

2. To assemble: Place a lavash on a large piece of wax paper or foil. (This is a crumbly filling, so the wrap holds better that way.) With a short end facing you, pile about half of the salad in a strip across the lavash, about a third of the way up from the bottom. Roll it up, curling the bread under with your fingers as you roll and being careful not to wrap the wax paper or foil into the spiral. Seal the ends. Complete the wraps with the remaining ingredients. Or, if you prefer,

prepare all at once, assembly-line style. Cut in half on the bias. Peel down the wax paper or foil as you eat.
MAKES 2 WRAPS

Substitutions
Use warmed large burrito-size flour tortillas instead of lavash. Dill may be substituted for mint.

Make Ahead/Take Away
Sealed in plastic wrap, wax paper, or foil and refrigerated, the wraps keep well for up to 3 hours. (They will get a tad soggy, but the flavors will be bright.) Or, if you prefer, chill the salad and dressing separately up to a day in advance, then assemble right before eating. Serve cold.

Panzanella

 When local tomatoes are at their peak, this wrap, based on the Italian tomato-bread salad, is sheer ambrosia—ripe tomatoes with basil and garlic, nestled in a flatbread that sops up the flavorful juices as fast as you can eat it. If you prefer not to turn on your broiler in the summer heat, crisp one side of the pita in a large, heavy dry skillet.

2 ripe medium tomatoes, coarsely chopped
3 tablespoons diced red onion
10 fresh basil leaves, torn into 2 or 3 pieces each
2 tablespoons fruity olive oil, plus extra for brushing the pita
2 teaspoons drained capers
2 teaspoons red wine vinegar
salt and freshly ground pepper to taste
2 pocketless pitas
2 handfuls of mixed baby greens

1. Combine the tomatoes, onion, basil, olive oil, capers, vinegar, and salt and pepper in a medium bowl. Allow to sit for 15 minutes to 1 hour.

2. To assemble: Preheat the broiler. Brush one side of each pita with olive oil. Broil, oiled side up, until they start to crisp slightly but do not turn brittle, about 1 minute. Place each pita bread, crisp side down, on a 12-inch square of foil. Top each pita with a handful of greens and half the tomato salad down the center. Wrap into a cone shape, using the foil as support and to seal the bottom. Peel down the foil as you eat.

MAKES 2 WRAPS

Substitutions
For a pretty variation, use half red and half yellow tomatoes.

Make Ahead/Take Away
Step 1 can be done up to 24 hours in advance and the mixture refrigerated. Leave out for 15 minutes before assembling, then reseason with salt and pepper to taste before wrapping. The wrap will be even juicier this way, so have plenty of napkins ready. Serve immediately after assembling, at room temperature or cold.

Et Tu Brute Roll

 Caesar salads have made a big comeback, becoming frequent staples on all sorts of restaurant menus, often served with grilled chicken or shrimp. This twist with strips of filet mignon and anchovy, beats them all.

1 tablespoon fresh lemon juice
1 garlic clove, minced
2 teaspoons Dijon mustard
¼ teaspoon coarsely ground pepper
2 tablespoons olive oil
½ pound filet mignon, cut into 2 medallions
4 cups lightly packed shredded romaine lettuce leaves
6 anchovies, cut in half
4 thin slices of red onion, separated into rings
¼ cup coarsely grated Parmesan or Asiago cheese
2 lavash rectangles

1. Combine the lemon juice, garlic, mustard, and pepper in large bowl. Whisk in the olive oil. Set aside.

2. Heat a nonstick pan over high heat. Add the filet and sear, turning once or twice, until it has reached the desired doneness, 2 to 4 minutes on each side. Remove to a cutting board. Allow to stand for 10 minutes, then slice.

3. Add the lettuce, anchovies, onion, and Parmesan to the bowl and toss. Add the sliced filet and toss again.

4. To assemble: Place a lavash on a large piece of wax paper or foil. (This is a crumbly filling, so the wrap holds better that way.) With a short end facing you, pile about half of the salad in a strip across the lavash, about a third of the way up from the bottom. Roll it up, curling the bread under with your fingers as you roll and being careful not to wrap the wax paper or foil into the spiral. Seal the ends. Complete the wraps with the remaining ingredients. Or, if you prefer, prepare all at once, assembly-line style. Cut in half on the bias. Peel down the wax paper or foil as you eat.

MAKES 2 WRAPS

Make Ahead/Take Away

The salad, dressing and cooked, unsliced meat can be held up to a day in advance in the refrigerator. The assembled wraps, sealed in wax paper, foil, or plastic wrap and refrigerated, keep well for up to 3 hours before serving. Serve room temperature or cold.

Steak Salad with Chimichurri Sauce

 This colorful dish is a meat eater's dream: warm bread topped with slices of juicy steak and rounds of white onion in ribbons of piquant South American green sauce. Use your favorite cut of tender steak.

1 cup packed fresh parsley leaves
1 garlic clove, peeled
4 very thin slices of onion
¼ cup olive oil, plus extra for brushing pita
1 tablespoon fresh lime juice
1 teaspoon white vinegar
generous pinch of sugar
salt and freshly ground black pepper to taste
1 12- to 16-ounce steak, such as strip or sirloin
4 pocketless pitas

1. In a blender, combine the parsley, garlic, and 1 onion slice. With the motor running, pour the ¼ cup olive oil and ¼ cup water through the feed tube. Add the lime juice, vinegar, and sugar. Blend until smooth. Season with salt and pepper.

2. Heat a grill or lightly oiled skillet to medium-high heat and cook the steak, turning twice, until it has reached the desired doneness, about 5 to 10 minutes total. Remove to a cutting board, season with salt and pepper, and wrap lightly in foil.

3. To assemble: Brush one side of each pita with olive oil. Heat, oiled side down, on a grill or skillet until crisp but not brittle, about 1 minute each. Thinly slice the steak. Place each of the 4 warm pitas, soft side up, in the center of a plate. Overlap one quarter of the steak slices on top of each pita. Using a spoon, drizzle the green sauce on top. Break the remaining onion slices into rounds or crescents and scatter on top. Serve with extra green sauce on the side. (If you prefer, assemble portable wraps instead. Lay the pita on a 12-inch square of foil; top with the sliced steak, onions, and sauce down the center, then roll it into a cone, rolling the bread and foil together, sealing the bottom with foil.)

MAKES 4 WRAPS

Make Ahead/Take Away
Best if served immediately.

Vietnamese Pork and Lettuce Rolls

 Try these subtle pork meatballs, set out on lettuce, with cucumber, mint, and dipping sauce, ready to be rolled into an unusual meal. They make an attractive appetizer or light lunch platter. Guests can assemble and roll their own.

Fish sauce can be purchased in the Asian section of the supermarket and keeps indefinitely. Jícama, a slightly sweet crisp root vegetable, adds a surprise crunch to the pork. I use the leftover jícama for an appetizer or snack, Mexican street vendor style, cut into wedges or sticks, then sprinkled lightly with cayenne pepper and fresh lime juice.

1 pound ground pork
⅔ cup finely chopped jícama
3 garlic cloves, minced
¾ teaspoon salt
1½ tablespoons sugar
1 teaspoon hot red pepper flakes
1 tablespoon dry sherry
2 tablespoons fresh lime juice
1 tablespoon rice wine vinegar
1 tablespoon fish sauce
1 tablespoon vegetable oil
24 small lettuce leaves, such as green leaf or Bibb
24 fresh mint leaves
2 Kirby cucumbers, peeled in stripes and sliced
6 to 8 strips of carrot, shaved with a peeler, for garnish

1. With your hands mix the pork, jícama, garlic, salt, 1½ teaspoons of the sugar, ¾ teaspoon of the hot red pepper flakes, and the sherry until combined thoroughly. Form into 1½-inch balls.

2. Preheat the oven to 200°F. Combine the lime juice, vinegar, fish sauce, remaining 1 tablespoon sugar, and remaining ¼ teaspoon hot red pepper flakes in a small bowl. Set aside.

3. Heat half the oil in a large nonstick skillet over medium-high heat. Brown about half the balls evenly, shaking the pan so they do not stick. Continue cooking just until they are cooked through, about 5 minutes, moving them around so they cook evenly. Set the balls on a heat-proof plate in the oven to keep warm, add the remaining oil to the skillet, and finish cooking the remaining balls.

4. To assemble: Serve the balls immediately on a large platter covered with the lettuce leaves. Scatter the mint, cucumber, and carrot over the top. To eat, roll the balls in lettuce with mint and cucumber. Dip the wraps in the sauce.

MAKES 24 WRAPS, SERVING ABOUT 5 TO 6 FOR LUNCH OR ABOUT 8 TO 10 AS AN APPETIZER

Make Ahead/Take Away

Make the dipping sauce and meatballs ahead of time and store in the refrigerator, well covered, for up to 1 day. When ready to serve, cook the meatballs and assemble the platter. Serve warm or at room temperature.

Mandarin Chicken Salad
with Radicchio

 Wild colors and vivid flavors in a meal-in-a-roll that's tasty warm, at room temperature, or even cold. Green peppercorns can be found near the capers in the condiments section of the supermarket.

2 boneless, skinless chicken breast halves, cut into 1-inch strips
1½ teaspoons green peppercorns, crushed
1 teaspoon ground coriander
salt to taste
1½ teaspoons olive oil
1 garlic clove, peeled and crushed
1 8-ounce can mandarin oranges in juice, drained and
   juice reserved
1 tablespoon red wine vinegar
8 radicchio leaves, thickest part of spine removed, stacked,
   rolled together, and cut into 1-inch strips
3 thin slices of Vidalia or red onion
4 large burrito-size flour tortillas

1. Rub the chicken with crushed green peppercorns; sprinkle with coriander and ⅛ teaspoon salt.

2. Heat the oil in a large nonstick pan over medium heat. Add the garlic and chicken breasts. Cook, stirring occasionally, for 5 to 7 minutes or until the chicken is just cooked through. Transfer the chicken to a medium bowl.

3. Add 2 tablespoons of the reserved mandarin orange juice and the vinegar to the pan and boil, watching closely, until it is reduced by half, about 1 minute. Pour over the chicken. Add ½ cup of the drained mandarin orange slices, reserv-

ing any remaining orange slices for another use, along with the radicchio and onion, and toss.

4. To assemble: Heat the tortillas, one at a time, directly on a gas flame, on a grill, or in a hot skillet, turning frequently, until hot and pliable, 5 to 15 seconds each. Or heat the tortillas, stacked, in the microwave (see page 19). Place a quarter of the salad in a thick horizontal strip across the bottom third of the tortillas, making sure the ingredients don't quite touch the edges. Fold in the two sides and roll the wrap away from you. Complete the wraps with the remaining ingredients. Or, if you prefer, prepare all at once, assembly-line style. Cut in half on the bias.

MAKES 4 WRAPS

Trim the Fat
This is a low-fat wrap.

Make Ahead/Take Away
Sealed in wax paper, foil, or plastic wrap and refrigerated, the wraps keep well for up to 4 hours. Serve at room temperature or cold.

Fall Salad Wrap

 This is one of my favorite wraps. In fact, the balance of nutty, sharp, and sweet drove me and my assistant, Katy, wild; we just couldn't stop eating it. Accompanied with cider and oatmeal cookies, it conjures up images of an autumn hike.

2 tablespoons olive oil
½ cup coarsely chopped walnuts
generous pinch of salt
½ pound sliced smoked turkey, cut into thin strips
4 cups loosely packed chopped escarole leaves
2 ripe pears, cored and diced
⅓ cup raisins
⅓ cup crumbled blue cheese
4 teaspoons fresh lemon juice
4 lavash rectangles

1. Heat the oil in a medium skillet. Add the nuts and salt, and cook, stirring frequently, until the nuts are fragrant but not browned, about 2 to 4 minutes.

2. Add the nuts and oil to a large bowl with the turkey, escarole, pears, raisins, blue cheese, and lemon juice. Toss to coat well.

3. To assemble: Place a lavash on a large piece of wax paper or foil. (This is a crumbly filling, so the wrap holds better that way.) With a short end facing you, pile about a quarter of the salad in a strip across the lavash, about a third of the way up from the bottom. Roll it up, compressing the salad, curling the bread under with your fingers as you roll, and being careful not to wrap the wax paper or foil into the spiral.

Seal the ends. Complete the wraps with the remaining ingredients. Or, if you prefer, prepare all at once, assembly-line style. Cut in half on the bias. Peel down the wax paper or foil as you eat.

MAKES 4 WRAPS

Substitutions

Replace the lavash with large burrito-size flour tortillas. Use regular sliced turkey in place of the smoked and try pecans instead of the walnuts.

Make Ahead/Take Away

Sealed in plastic wrap, wax paper, or foil and refrigerated, these wraps keep well for up to 1 day. Serve warm, cold, or at room temperature.

Sardinian Roll

People love or hate sardines. If you fall into the latter category, turn the page; otherwise this wrap is for you. I come from a family of sardine lovers. When I was little, my father used to keep sardine tins by the case in our suburban basement. I always shared his passion for the little fish, and open-faced sardine sandwiches, with slices of sweet onion, freshly ground pepper, and a squeeze of lemon, are still comfort food for me. This fabulous wrap version makes an almost instant lunch or snack. (Of the commonly available brands of sardines on the market, I prefer King Oscar packed in olive oil.)

2 lavash rectangles
4 large green leaf lettuce leaves
1 3¾-ounce tin sardines packed in olive oil
3 to 4 thin slices Vidalia onion or to taste
4 teaspoons fresh lemon juice
Freshly ground pepper to taste

To assemble: Place each lavash on a large piece of wax paper or foil. (This is a crumbly filling, so the wrap holds better that way.) With a long side of both lavash rectangles facing you, cover each with 2 lettuce leaves. Divide half the sardines and half the onions equally over the lettuce. Drizzle each with a little olive oil from the tin, 2 teaspoons lemon juice, followed by a generous grind of fresh pepper. Roll it up away from you, curling the bread under with your fingers as you roll and being careful not to wrap the wax paper or foil into the spiral. Seal the ends. Complete the wraps with the remaining ingredients. Or, if you prefer, prepare all at once, assembly-line style. Cut in half on the bias. Peel down the wax paper or foil as you eat.

MAKES 4 SMALL WRAPS

Substitutions

If Vidalia onions are unavailable, substitute 2 slices of a Spanish onion. If lavash is unavailable, replace with large burrito-size flour tortillas, warmed (see page 19).

Make Ahead/Take Away

Best eaten immediately.

Grilled Swordfish Salad

 This refreshing salad requires a flavorful olive oil. If you don't have an outdoor grill or an indoor grill pan (page 15), the swordfish may be broiled.

2½ tablespoons fruity olive oil
juice and finely grated zest of 1 lemon
salt and freshly ground pepper to taste
¾ pound swordfish steak
1⅓ cups cooked white rice
2 plum tomatoes, seeded and roughly chopped
¼ cup chopped fresh dill
¼ cup chopped red onion, optional
1 tablespoon drained capers, chopped
1 garlic clove, minced
4 lavash rectangles
8 to 12 small spinach leaves

1. Combine 1 tablespoon olive oil, half the lemon juice, and the salt and pepper in a shallow bowl. Add the swordfish and marinate at room temperature for 20 minutes, turning 2 or 3 times.

2. Meanwhile, combine the rice, tomatoes, dill, onion, capers, garlic, lemon zest, remaining lemon juice, and 1½ tablespoons olive oil. Season with salt and pepper.

3. Heat a lightly oiled grill pan or outdoor grill to medium-high. Grill the swordfish, basting frequently with the marinade, until just cooked through, 3 to 5 minutes per side, depending on thickness. Remove from heat and allow to cool, then flake into the rice salad and toss.

4. To assemble: Place a lavash on a large piece of wax paper or foil. (This is a crumbly filling, so the wrap holds better that way.) Cover with a layer of spinach leaves. With a short end facing you, pile about a quarter of the salad in a strip across the lavash, about a third of the way up from the bottom. Roll it up, curling the bread under with your fingers as you roll. Complete the wraps with the remaining ingredients. Or, if you prefer, prepare all at once, assembly-line style. Cut in half on the bias. Peel down the wax paper or foil as you eat.

MAKES 4 WRAPS

Substitutions

Use salmon or tuna instead of swordfish, heated large burrito-size flour tortillas for the lavash.

Trim the Fat

This is a low-fat wrap if all gray fat is trimmed from the fish.

Make Ahead/Take Away

Sealed in wax paper, foil, or plastic wrap and refrigerated, these wraps keep well for up to 8 hours.

Riviera Roll

 Capture the sunny flavors of the south of France in this lusty alternative to the traditional tuna sandwich. Despite the long list of ingredients, assembly is quick, no cooking is required, and most everything can be kept on hand in your pantry. The dressing, a caper anchoïade, also makes a great warm-weather dip with vegetables and crusty bread.

**¼ cup olive oil, preferably extra-virgin, plus extra for
  brushing pita
4 teaspoons fresh lemon juice
1½ tablespoons drained capers
1 large garlic clove, minced
¾ teaspoon anchovy paste
½ teaspoon freshly ground pepper
1 12-ounce can or 2 6½-ounce cans tuna, packed in water and
  well drained
4 plum tomatoes, chopped
2 celery ribs, chopped
¼ cup chopped red onion
8 Kalamata olives, pitted and chopped
pinch of salt if necessary
4 pocketless pitas
about 24 fresh basil leaves**

1. Blend together ¼ cup of the olive oil, the lemon juice, 1 tablespoon of the capers, the garlic, anchovy paste, and pepper in a medium bowl.

2. Add the tuna, tomatoes, celery, red onion, olives, remaining 1½ teaspoons capers, and a pinch of salt if necessary (the olives, anchovy paste, and capers will probably provide plenty of salt). Toss gently to combine.

3. To assemble: Preheat the broiler. Brush one side of each pita with olive oil.

Broil, oiled side up, until they start to crisp slightly but do not turn brittle, about 1 minute. Place each pita bread, crisp side down, on a 12-inch square of foil. Top each with 6 or so basil leaves and a quarter of the tuna mixture in a strip down the middle. Wrap the pita into a cone shape, using the foil as support and to seal the bottom well. Peel down as you eat.

MAKES 4 WRAPS

Substitutions

Replace the canned tuna with cooked left-over fish or seafood.

To turn this into a Riviera Veggie Wrap, leave out the tuna, double the tomato, and add your favorite vegetables, like sliced cucumber and raw or roasted red pepper.

Trim the Fat

This is a low-fat wrap if both the olives and olive oil are cut in half and the anchovy paste is eliminated.

Make Ahead/Take Away

Make the salad mixture up to a day in advance and refrigerate. Let sit for 15 minutes at room temperature before assembling. Serve cold or at room temperature.

Coconut Curry Shrimp Salad

 A sauté of coconut, shrimp, and spices is transformed into a fiery shrimp salad, with a chewy coconut-yogurt dressing.

4 teaspoons vegetable oil
1 cup sweetened flaked coconut, toasted
2 teaspoons minced garlic
2 teaspoons minced peeled fresh ginger
1 jalapeño pepper or more to taste, seeded and minced
1 tablespoon curry powder or more to taste, preferably Madras
¼ teaspoon salt
8 to 10 ounces medium shrimp (about 24), peeled and deveined
⅔ cup plain yogurt
2 tablespoons fresh lime juice
3 cups shredded romaine lettuce
4 large burrito-size flour tortillas

1. In a large skillet, over medium-high heat, heat the oil, then add the coconut, garlic, ginger, jalapeño, curry, and salt and cook, stirring constantly, about 2 minutes. Add the shrimp and continue to stir (don't worry if the mixture seems dry), just until shrimp is cooked through, 4 to 5 minutes.

2. Remove from the heat and stir in the yogurt and lime juice, scraping up any browned bits from the bottom. Place the lettuce in a large bowl. Add the shrimp mixture and toss well.

3. To assemble: Heat the tortillas, one at a time, directly on a gas flame, on a grill, or in a hot skillet, turning frequently, until hot and pliable, about 5 to 15 seconds each. Or heat, stacked, in the microwave (see page 19). Place a tortilla on top of a 12-inch square of foil. Place a quarter of the salad in a thick horizontal strip across the bottom third of the tortillas, making sure the ingredients don't quite touch the edges. Fold in the two sides and roll the wrap away from you, being careful not to roll the foil into the spiral. Seal the ends. Complete the wraps with the remaining ingredients. Or, if your prefer, prepare all at once, assembly-line style. Cut in half on the bias. Peel down the foil as you eat.

MAKES 4 WRAPS

Make Ahead/Take Away
Sealed in plastic wrap, wax paper, or foil, and refrigerated, these wraps keep well for up to half a day. Serve warm (after cooking) or cold. Do not reheat.

Shrimp Cucumber Sambal

 Sambal is a mixture of fruits or vegetables, seasoned with hot chilies and spices. This Southeast Asian-inspired sambal makes a refreshing nonfat summer wrap. If you purchase cooked shrimp and have leftover rice on hand, no cooking is required (to cook rice, see page 14). Fish sauce can be purchased in the Asian section of supermarkets or in specialty markets.

10 medium shrimp, cooked, peeled, deveined, and coarsely chopped
1 medium Kirby cucumber, finely chopped
¼ cup finely chopped red onion
3 tablespoons rice wine vinegar
2 tablespoons fresh lime juice
1 tablespoon fish sauce
1 tablespoon sugar
2 teaspoons chopped fresh mint leaves
1 to 2 jalapeño peppers, to taste, minced
1 teaspoon ground coriander
¼ teaspoon salt or to taste
1 cup cooked white rice
2 green leaf lettuce leaves, torn into bite-size pieces
2 large burrito-size flour tortillas

1. In a large bowl, combine the shrimp, cucumber, onion, vinegar, lime juice, fish sauce, sugar, mint leaves, jalapeños, coriander, and salt. Let sit for 5 minutes. Add the rice and lettuce. Toss to combine.

2. Heat the tortillas, one at a time, directly on a gas flame, on a grill, or in a hot skillet, turning frequently, until hot and pliable, 5 to 15 seconds each. Or heat, stacked, in the microwave (see page 19). Lay each tortilla on top of a 12-inch square of foil. Place half the sambal in a thick horizontal strip across the bottom third of each tortilla, making sure the ingredients don't quite touch the edges. Fold in the two sides and roll the wrap away from you, being careful not to wrap the foil into the spiral. Cut in half on the bias. Peel down the foil as you eat.

MAKES 2 WRAPS

Trim the Fat
This is a low-fat wrap.

Make Ahead/Take Away
You can prepare the sambal up to 1 hour ahead and refrigerate, but assemble the wraps just before eating. Serve cold.

Smoked Trout–Avocado Salad Cups

 This summery, savory salad can be wrapped and eaten out of hand for an appetizer. Alternatively, for a sophisticated lunch or first course, divide the salad among 4 to 6 large leaves instead of 10 small leaves and eat with a knife and fork. Boneless smoked trout fillets are often available, prewrapped, in the fish section of the supermarket or a good deli. If unavailable, smoked trout can also be purchased whole and skinned and boned. (Your fishmonger will sometimes do this for you.)

2 skinless trout fillets (about ½ pound total), broken into bite-size pieces
1 ripe avocado, peeled, pitted, and diced
1 medium tomato, diced
½ cup plain yogurt
1 to 1½ tablespoons drained horseradish or to taste
10 small cup-shaped inner Boston lettuce leaves
1 tablespoon chopped chives or scallion greens

1. In a medium bowl, combine the trout, avocado, and tomato. Toss gently to combine.

2. In a small bowl, stir together the yogurt and horseradish.

3. To assemble: Place the leaves on a platter. Equally divide the horseradish sauce among the leaves, spreading it along the bottom of each. Top with the smoked trout salad, mounding it up inside each leaf. Sprinkle with chives or scallion greens. Alternatively, instead of spreading the sauce inside each leaf, you can serve it on the side and let the diners help themselves.

MAKES 10 APPETIZER WRAPS, 4 LUNCH WRAPS, OR 4 TO 6 FIRST-COURSE WRAPS

Substitutions

I like rich flavor in the avocado only. But if you like the decadent flavor of sour cream in the dressing as well, up to 2 tablespoons of the yogurt may be replaced by sour cream.

Take Along/Make Ahead

The salad, without the avocado and the horseradish cream, will keep in the refrigerator for up to a day. Before serving, add the avocado and assemble. Serve cold or at room temperature.

5 vegetable wraps

I'm forever in awe of simple vegetables; their variety of flavors and textures astounds me—from woodsy wild mushrooms to sweet sugar snaps. In this chapter they are the stars, taking center stage in vegetable wraps that span the seasons.

We've all become acutely aware that we should eat more vegetables because they are so healthful. Luckily they taste great too. For those two reasons, vegetable-packed wraps dominate this book. All of the wraps in this chapter are vegetarian except the Sweet Potato and Shiitake Mushroom Roll. Many wraps in other chapters are jammed with veggies as well—be sure to check out Chapter 4 (salads) in particular.

The first rule of cooking with vegetables is to go for what's best in the market. Remember that seasonal produce is usually the most readily available, the freshest, and often the least expensive. When possible, buy locally harvested vegetables for peak flavor (and to support your local

farmers, ensuring more harvests next season). Because freshness is top priority, make substitutions when necessary, checking the ingredients list for ideas about what vegetables would work in the dish, as well as the substitution notes below the recipe. Swap delicate vegetables for delicate vegetables, hearty ones for hearty ones, but don't be afraid to experiment. Mostly, if you see something fresh that cries out to be eaten, buy it!

Not only does the fresh produce taste better, but eating seasonal food in its natural context is more satisfying. Hearty Veggie-Pesto Spiral should be savored on a snowy afternoon or Corny Avocado Taco on a late-summer day, while the corn is still plump and sweet.

If you have already discovered the possibilities of the veggie wrap via take-out, wait until you taste your homemade vegetable wrap, made from a wider variety of fresh vegetables chosen by you and cooked to taste.

VEGETABLE

Corny Avocado Taco

Crisp Broccoli Rabe "Manicotti"

Antipasto Wrap

Good to Eat Beet, Hazelnut, and Gorgonzola Wrap

Hearty Veggie-Pesto Spiral

Roasted Garlic Summer Roll

Seventies Roll

Smoky Eggplant Gyro

Steamed Vegetable Wrap Two Ways

Thyme Roasted Vegetables with Chèvre

Wrap-tatouille

Sweet Potato and Shiitake Mushroom Roll

Wild Mushroom Wrapture

Thai Noodle Veggie Wrap

Veggie Pizza Takes a Spin

Corny Avocado Taco

 In Mexico, one of my favorite treats is to squeeze sweet limes onto flavorful avocados, folded into aromatic corn tortillas. Here I've added some fresh corn kernels to create an instant make-and-eat vegetarian taco that hits the spot. Look for the best corn tortillas available. In my neck of the woods in New England, I like El Toro brand, found in some supermarkets, but any brand that really smells of corn will do.

2 corn tortillas
1 ripe small avocado, preferably Hass, at room temperature, peeled and pitted
2 teaspoons fresh lime juice
1 small ear of corn, kernels removed, or leftover cooked corn
about 10 large cilantro leaves
salt to taste
hot sauce to taste

To assemble: Wet your hands and rub them across the tortillas. Heat together, stacked in a hot skillet, turning frequently, until they become soft, about 1 minute. With a fork, mash half the avocado a little with a fork right into the center of each tortilla, just to break it up a bit. Top the avocado with half the lime juice, corn, and cilantro and salt and hot sauce to taste. Roll.
MAKES 2 WRAPS

Make Ahead/Take Away
Best served immediately.

Crisp Broccoli Rabe "Manicotti"

 If you like bitter greens, as I do, this wrap is for you. No pasta here, but an oven-crisped flatbread wrapper filled with broccoli rabe and cheese and accompanied by a thick, naturally sweet sun-dried tomato sauce.

1 bunch of broccoli rabe, tough stems removed, chopped
3 cups coarsely grated fontina cheese (about 8 ounces)
½ cup coarsely grated Romano cheese
4 garlic cloves, finely minced
½ teaspoon hot red pepper flakes
4 large burrito-size flour tortillas
1 tablespoon olive oil, preferably fruity
1 8-ounce can Italian-style stewed tomatoes
5 sun-dried tomato halves packed in oil

1. Preheat the oven to 425°F. (If you like, reserve 2 tablespoons of broccoli rabe greens, finely chopped, for garnish.) Toss the broccoli rabe, fontina, Romano, 3 of the garlic cloves, and the hot red pepper flakes in a large bowl.

2. To assemble: Stack the tortillas, wrap them in foil, and heat in the oven just until warm and pliable, about 2 to 4 minutes. (Be careful not to overheat, or they will become brittle.) Or heat the tortillas, one at a time, in a hot skillet, turning frequently, for 5 to 15 seconds each. Heap a quarter of the broccoli rabe mixture in the center of the tortilla. Fold in the sides and roll. Repeat with the remaining wraps. Place a lightly oiled baking sheet in the oven for 5 minutes. Carefully place the wraps on the sheet, seam sides down. Bake until browned on one side, turn, and brown until very crisp on the second side, 12 to 15 minutes total.

3. To make the sauce: While the wraps are cooking, heat the oil and remaining garlic clove in a small pot over medium heat. When the garlic starts to smell aromatic, after about 1 minute, add the stewed tomatoes and their juices and the sun-dried tomato halves. Simmer, covered, until the sun-dried tomatoes are very soft, about 5 minutes. In a food processor or blender, blend until smooth, adding up to 2 tablespoons water, if necessary, to bring the sauce to the desired consistency. Return to the pot and keep warm until the manicotti wraps are ready. Serve with sauce spooned over each wrap and, if you wish, a sprinkling of the reserved broccoli rabe greens.
MAKES 4 WRAPS

If you prefer, use whole wheat mountain bread instead of tortillas. This will make 6 wraps.

Make Ahead/Take Away
The sauce can be made a day ahead of time; refrigerate it and reheat while the wraps are baking. The wraps can be assembled up to an hour before baking. Serve warm, within 15 minutes of cooking.

Antipasto Wrap

 An appetizer or lunch that can be assembled quickly from pantry items—great for last-minute guests or midnight snacks.

½ cup coarsely chopped drained marinated artichoke hearts
¼ cup coarsely chopped red onion
3 tablespoons coarsely chopped drained jarred roasted red peppers
5 imported black olives, pitted and coarsely chopped
2 teaspoons fresh lemon juice
1 pita pocket, split horizontally into 2 rounds
4 to 6 slices fontina or Swiss cheese

To assemble: Preheat the broiler. Divide the artichoke hearts, red onion, red peppers, olives, and lemon juice equally over each pita round, leaving a 1-inch border. Top each with half the sliced cheese. Broil just until the cheese is melted. Roll immediately. Slice into halves or thirds on the diagonal with a serrated knife. Serve hot.

MAKES 2 WRAPS, SERVING 2 AS LUNCH OR 2 TO 3 AS AN APPETIZER

Make Ahead/Take Away
Best served immediately.

Good to Eat Beet, Hazelnut, and Gorgonzola Wrap

 This sophisticated wrap includes both quick-roasted beets and their greens. Choose beets with pert, healthy-looking greens still attached.

1 bunch of beets (about 1½ pounds, 4 to 6 medium beets)
1 tablespoon vegetable oil
¼ cup chopped hazelnuts
4 thin slices of red onion
4 teaspoons red wine vinegar
3 large burrito-size flour tortillas
¼ cup Gorgonzola cheese at room temperature

1. Preheat the oven to 450°F. Cut the beet greens from the beets. Cut off and discard the stems. Wash and dry about 20 leaves, tearing each into 2 or 3 pieces, and set aside. Cut the root ends off the beets and peel, using a vegetable peeler. Slice the beets into ¼-inch rounds and toss with 1 teaspoon of the oil. Lay out on a lightly oiled baking pan in a single layer. Roast until fork-tender, turning once, 15 to 20 minutes.

2. When the beets are done, heat the remaining 2 teaspoons oil in a large skillet over medium heat. Add the hazelnuts and red onion and cook, stirring frequently, until the nuts are toasted lightly, 3 to 4 minutes, watching closely to avoid burning the nuts. Add the beet greens and vinegar and toss frequently until the greens start to wilt, 1 to 2 minutes.

3. To assemble: Stack the tortillas and wrap in foil, then heat in the oven just until warm and pliable, 2 to 4 minutes. (Be careful not to overcook, or they will become brittle.) Or heat the tortillas, one at a time, directly on a gas flame, on a grill, or in a hot skillet, turning frequently, until hot and pliable, 5 to 15 seconds each. Spread a tortilla with 1 tablespoon of the gorgonzola, leaving a 1-inch border. Distribute a quarter of the greens, nuts, and beets in a thick horizontal strip across the bottom third of the tortilla, making sure the ingredients don't quite touch the edges. Fold in the two sides and roll the wrap away from you. Complete the wraps with the remaining ingredients. Or, if you prefer, prepare all at once, assembly-line style. Cut in half on the bias.

MAKES 3 WRAPS

Substitutions

Chopped hazelnuts in bags can usually be found with other nuts in the supermarket. If not, replace them with walnuts or pecans.

Trim the Fat

With the amount of cheese and hazelnuts reduced by half, this is a low-fat wrap.

Make Ahead/Take Away

The beets can be roasted up to 3 days before the wrap is assembled and stored in the refrigerator. The colorful beets bleed a little once the wrap is assembled, but that will not affect the flavor. Well sealed in wax paper, foil, or plastic wrap, and refrigerated, the wraps will keep for up to 3 hours. Unseal and heat each wrap in the microwave, covered with a shallow bowl to keep it moist, for about 1 minute. Serve warm or at room temperature.

Hearty Veggie-Pesto Spiral

 This twist of pretty colors celebrates underutilized and often unappreciated winter vegetables. Roasting deepens their flavors, which are complemented by a parsley-walnut pesto. During the fall and winter months, peeled and seeded butternut squash is often available at your greengrocer or in the produce section of your supermarket.

1 pound celery root, peeled and cut into ½-inch cubes (2 cups)
3 tablespoons olive oil
**2 leeks, root and tough greens discarded, rinsed, and cut into about
    1-inch slices (2 cups)**
**1 pound medium turnips, peeled and cut into about ¾-inch cubes (2
    cups)**
1 pound peeled butternut squash, cut into about ¾-inch cubes (2 cups)
4 teaspoons fresh lemon juice
¼ cup vegetable or chicken stock
½ cup chopped walnuts
1 garlic clove, minced
2 tablespoons grated Parmesan cheese
2 cups loosely packed fresh parsley leaves
⅛ teaspoon salt
⅛ teaspoon freshly ground pepper
4 lavash rectangles

1. Preheat the oven to 425°F. Toss the celery root with 1 tablespoon of the olive oil in a roasting pan large enough to hold all the vegetables in 1 layer. Roast for 10 minutes. Remove from the oven. Add the leeks, turnips, and squash and toss well. Continue roasting, shaking occasionally to prevent sticking, until the vegetables are fork-tender and slightly browned, about 20 to 30 minutes. Remove from the oven and toss with 2 teaspoons of the lemon juice and the stock.

2. To make the pesto: While the vegetables are roasting, toast the walnuts in the oven on a baking sheet for 2 to 4 minutes, watching them carefully to prevent burning. Place ¼ cup of the nuts in a food processor along with the garlic and Parmesan and blend, scraping down the sides. Add the parsley, the remaining 2 teaspoons lemon juice, the remaining 2 tablespoons olive oil, and the salt and pepper. Blend well, stopping again to scrape down the sides if necessary, until smooth.

3. To assemble: With a short end facing you, spread 2 tablespoons pesto evenly over an entire lavash rectangle. Leaving a 1-inch border, sprinkle a quarter of the roasted vegetables evenly over the pesto, followed by 1 tablespoon of the reserved nuts. Roll it up. Complete the rest of the wraps with the remaining ingredients. Or, if you prefer, prepare them all at once, assembly-line style. Cut in half on the bias.

MAKES 4 WRAPS

Substitutions
This recipe calls for my favorite assortment of winter vegetables, but feel free to use 8 cups total of any hearty vegetables, including parsnips, carrots, potatoes, and sweet potatoes.

Shortcuts
Use store-bought pesto—not quite as good, but faster and still tasty.

Make Ahead/Take Away
Well sealed in wax paper or foil, these keep well at room temperature for up to 3 hours but are best eaten immediately, warm or at room temperature.

Roasted Garlic Summer Roll

 This makes a fine picnic lunch, salad course, or accompaniment at a cookout. Don't worry about the quantity of garlic used here; the flavor mellows considerably with roasting to create an aromatic spread for these Italian-style rolls. Fresh mozzarella can be found in the deli section of most supermarkets or at specialty stores.

2 whole heads of garlic
2 tablespoons olive oil, preferably extra-virgin
1 tablespoon red wine vinegar
4 small taco-size flour tortillas
salt and freshly ground pepper to taste
1 bunch of arugula, tough ends trimmed
5 ounces fresh mozzarella cheese, sliced
1 ripe tomato, sliced, stacked, and cut into quarters
8 Kalamata olives, pitted and chopped

1. Preheat the oven to 375°F. Cut off the top end of each head of garlic to expose the cloves generously. Lay them on a large sheet of foil. Drizzle the 2 bulbs with 1 tablespoon of the olive oil and wrap to enclose. Roast until soft and slightly browned, about 45 minutes. Remove from the oven. When cool enough to handle, squeeze the garlic out of its paper skin into a small bowl. Stir in the remaining tablespoon of oil and the vinegar.

2. To assemble: Stack the tortillas, wrap in foil, and heat in the oven until warm and pliable, 5 to 10 minutes. (Do not overheat, or they will become brittle.) Or heat the tortillas, one at a time, directly on a gas flame or in a hot skillet, turning frequently, until hot and pliable, about 5 to 15 seconds each. Spread a tortilla with a quarter of the roasted garlic mixture, leaving a ½-inch border. Sprinkle with salt and pepper. Distribute the arugula, fresh mozzarella, tomato, and olives in a thick horizontal strip across the bottom third of the tortilla, making sure the ingredients don't quite touch the edges, then roll the wrap away from you. Complete the wraps with the remaining ingredients. Or, if you prefer, prepare all at once, assembly-line style. Cut in half on the bias.

MAKES 4 SMALL WRAPS

Substitutions
Use smoked mozzarella instead of fresh.

Trim the Fat

Omit the mozzarella or use a low- or reduced-fat version and cut the oil in half.

Make Ahead/Take Away

The bright, clean flavors in these wraps are best assembled close to eating time. Still, they are tasty when assembled up to 2 hours ahead; just wrap in wax paper, foil, or plastic wrap and refrigerate. Serve at room temperature.

Seventies Roll

 The fashion of this decade has returned, so why not the food? In the early seventies, when I was first living on my own, the ingredients in this wrap, often supplemented with cheese, were a vegetarian favorite.

1 small ripe avocado, preferably Hass
1 tablespoon fresh lime juice
1 small garlic clove, minced
pinch of salt
4 rounds of whole-wheat mountain bread
4 large romaine leaves, broken in half
1 large tomato, sliced
about 20 to 25 slices of pickled jalapeño peppers or to taste
1 cup alfalfa sprouts or sprout mix
4 slices of onion, separated into rings

1. Peel and pit the avocado, then coarsely mash with a fork in a small bowl with the lime juice, garlic, and salt.

2. To assemble: Heat the mountain bread, one at a time, in a hot skillet, turning frequently, just until hot and pliable, about 15 seconds each. Or stack the mountain bread and heat in the microwave (see page 19). Lay a mountain bread round on a piece of wax paper or foil. (This will help hold the wrap together.) Spread the center of each with about a quarter of the avocado mixture, leaving a 1- to 2-inch border. Top the avocado mixture with a quarter of the lettuce, tomato, jalapeño, sprouts, and onion. Roll it up, curling the bread under with your fingers as you roll and being careful not to wrap the wax paper or foil into the spiral. Complete the wraps with the remaining ingredients. Or, if you prefer, prepare all at once, assembly-line style. Cut in half on the bias. Peel down the wax paper or foil as you eat.
MAKES 4 WRAPS

Substitutions
Add thinly sliced or shredded Cheddar or any kind of cheese. To break with tradition, add sliced meat, such as turkey or ham.

Trim the Fat
To reduce the fat, cut the avocado in half and double the tomato.

Make Ahead/Take Away
Sealed in wax paper, foil, or plastic wrap and refrigerated, these wraps keep well for up to 6 days. Serve cold or at room temperature.

Smoky Eggplant Gyro

 Eggplant and scallions take well to grilling. Try this as a satisfying alternative to the traditional meat gyro.

3 tablespoons red wine vinegar
2 tablespoons soy sauce
1½ tablespoons sugar
3 tablespoons olive oil, plus extra for brushing pita
1 large eggplant, sliced into ½-inch rounds
8 scallions, root ends trimmed
1 large bunch of watercress, tough ends trimmed
salt to taste
4 pocketless pitas

1. Blend the vinegar, soy sauce, and sugar in a large bowl and whisk in the olive oil. Remove half the dressing to a small bowl and set aside. Toss the eggplant and scallions with the remaining dressing in the large bowl.

2. Preheat an indoor grill to high or an outdoor grill to medium. Cook the eggplant and scallions, in batches if necessary, turning occasionally, until soft, about 3 minutes on each side for the eggplant and 3 minutes total for the scallions. Alternatively, you can broil the vegetables for approximately the same times. Toss the vegetables with the watercress and the reserved dressing. (The watercress will wilt.) Season with salt if desired.

3. To assemble: Brush one side of each pita with oil and grill, oiled side down, until slightly crisp but not brittle, about 1 minute. Lay a pita on a 12-inch square sheet of foil, crispy side down. Spoon a quarter of the eggplant mixture in a strip down the center of each pita. Roll the pita and foil together into a cone, using the foil as support and to seal the bottom. Complete the remaining wraps. Or, if you prefer, prepare all at once, assembly-line style. Peel down the foil as you eat.
MAKES 4 WRAPS

Trim the Fat
To make this a low-fat wrap, skip brushing the pitas with olive oil and cut the rest of the oil in half.

Make Ahead/Take Away
The eggplant and scallions may be cooked the day before, reheated in the microwave, for about 1 minute, then tossed with the watercress and remaining dressing. To prepare the wraps, heat the pitas and assemble as described. Serve at once, hot or at room temperature.

Steamed Vegetable Wrap Two Ways

 A light, healthy wrap, jammed with tender-crisp vegetables. Even if you're not a tofu fan, you'll enjoy the smooth dressings—a choice of Lemon-Dill or Thai. They also make good dips for crudités. Fish sauce can be found in the Asian section of the supermarket, and in specialty stores.

LEMON-DILL DRESSING

3 scallions, white and green parts separated and sliced
1 10.5-ounce box soft or silken tofu, or equivalent, drained
¼ cup packed fresh dill sprigs
1 tablespoon fresh lemon juice
1 tablespoon rice wine vinegar
1 teaspoon Dijon mustard
¼ teaspoon salt
⅛ teaspoon freshly ground pepper

THAI DRESSING

1 teaspoon vegetable oil
1½ tablespoons grated peeled fresh ginger
1 jalapeño pepper, seeded and coarsely chopped
1 scallion white and green parts separated and sliced
1 teaspoon curry powder
1 10¼-ounce box soft or silken tofu, or equivalent, drained
⅓ cup packed cilantro leaves
2 tablespoons fresh lime juice
1 tablespoon fish sauce or soy sauce
1 teaspoon sugar

THE VEGETABLES

1½ cups sliced peeled carrots
3 cups small broccoli florets
1½ cups snow peas, stacked and sliced lengthwise
6 white or whole-wheat rounds of mountain bread

1. Choose either the Lemon-Dill or Thai dressing.

To make the Lemon-Dill Dressing:
Place the scallion whites in a food processor and pulse to chop finely. Add the tofu, dill, lemon juice, vinegar, mustard, salt, and pepper. Pulse until well combined, scraping down the sides if necessary. Let sit for at least 15 minutes before using to let the flavors marry.

To make the Thai Dressing:
In a skillet, heat the vegetable oil, ginger, jalapeño, scallion whites, and curry powder together over medium heat, stirring constantly, until the curry smells very aromatic, about 1 minute. Scrape into a food processor and pulse to combine. Add the tofu, cilantro, lime juice, fish sauce, and sugar. Process until smooth, about 30 seconds. Allow to sit for at least an hour before using so the spices can marry.

2. Place the carrots, topped with the broccoli and then the snow peas, into a steamer over boiling water. Cover the pot tightly, and allow to steam until the vegetables are tender-crisp, about 5 minutes. Run cold water over the vegetables until they are cold. Place on a dish towel to drain and dry.

3. To assemble: Heat the mountain bread, one at a time, in a hot skillet, just until hot and pliable, 5 to 15 seconds each. Place each round on a large square of wax paper (this will help hold the wrap together). Place about a sixth of the vegetables in a strip across the center of a round of bread. Top with about a sixth of either the Lemon Dill or Thai Dressing. Fold the bottom edge of the mountain bread up to cover the filling and roll away from you, being careful not to wrap the wax paper into the spiral. Complete the remaining wraps. Cut in half on the bias.
MAKES 6 WRAPS

Substitutions
Use your favorite vegetables, like cauliflower or asparagus.

Trim the Fat
This is a low-fat wrap; the Lemon Dill Dressing is slightly lower in fat.

Make Ahead/Take Away
Both dressings keep well for up to a day, covered, in the refrigerator. Sealed in wax paper, foil, or plastic and refrigerated, the wraps keep well for up to a day. Serve at room temperature or cold.

Thyme Roasted Vegetables with Chèvre

 Robust harvest vegetables and tangy goat cheese make this an ideal late summer or early fall wrap.

2 red bell peppers, cored, seeded, and sliced into rings
1 medium eggplant, sliced into ½-inch rounds
1 small zucchini, sliced
2 red onions, sliced into thick rings
2 tablespoons olive oil
5 fresh thyme sprigs or ⅛ teaspoon dried thyme leaves
1 teaspoon balsamic vinegar
1 garlic clove, minced
½ teaspoon salt
½ teaspoon freshly ground pepper
4 white rounds of mountain bread
½ cup fresh chèvre at room temperature

1. Preheat the oven to 450°F. Toss the peppers, eggplant, zucchini, onions, oil, thyme, vinegar, garlic, salt, and pepper in a large bowl. Spread in one layer on a baking sheet and roast, stirring twice and spreading out again to prevent sticking, until the eggplant is soft and the onions are brown, about 25 to 35 minutes. Remove the vegetables and set aside until they are cool enough to handle.

2. To assemble: Wrap the mountain bread in foil and heat in the oven until warm and pliable, about 3 to 5 minutes. Or heat in a hot skillet, one at a time, turning frequently, until hot and pliable, about 5 to 15 seconds each. Spread 1 round of mountain bread with 2 tablespoons chèvre, leaving a ½-inch border. Top with a quarter of the vegetables in a thick horizontal strip about a third of the way from the bottom. Roll away from you. Complete the wraps with the remaining ingredients. Or, if you prefer, prepare all at once, assembly-line style. Cut in half on the bias.

MAKES 4 WRAPS

Substitutions
You can use any of your favorite seasonal vegetables. In the spring I add asparagus but roast them for the last 10 minutes only.

Trim the Fat

This is a low-fat wrap if the oil and chèvre are cut in half. To replace the lost moisture, toss the cooled vegetables in 2 tablespoons of vegetable or chicken stock.

Make Ahead/Take Away

Terrific eaten at room temperature, warm, or even cold. Sealed in wax paper, foil, or plastic wrap, they keep at room temperature for up to 6 hours. Reheat just until warmed through, either sealed in foil in a preheated 350°F oven for 10 to 15 minutes or in the microwave, unsealed, for about 1 minute.

Wrap-tatouille

 In this portable version of the rustic Provençal ratatouille, vegetables are grilled and wrapped with a roasted tomato-olive tapenade. If grilling the vegetables in batches, store raw and cooked vegetables on either side of one large bowl, to reserve the savory juices. During the colder months you can cook the vegetables under a broiler, but you'll have to sacrifice that smoky grilled flavor.

2 large plum tomatoes, cut in half
1 small red bell pepper, cut into strips
1 small zucchini, cut lengthwise into ½-inch slices
1 small eggplant, cut into ½-inch slices
1 small onion, cut into ½-inch slices (about 4 slices)
2 tablespoons olive oil, preferably fruity
1 tablespoon balsamic vinegar
salt and freshly ground pepper to taste
8 Kalamata olives, pitted
1½ teaspoons drained capers
4 pocketless pitas
16 large basil leaves

1. Preheat an indoor grill to high or an outdoor grill to medium-high. (If neither is available, preheat a broiler.) Toss the tomatoes, pepper, zucchini, eggplant, and onion in the olive oil. Grill (or broil), in batches if necessary, until cooked through, about 3 to 4 minutes per side, with the exception of the tomatoes, which take only 1 to 2 minutes per side. Pull the vegetables off once they are soft and tender, reserving the tomatoes in the bowl of a food processor for the tapenade.

2. Toss the grilled vegetables except the tomatoes with the vinegar, salt, and pepper. Blend the olives and capers together with the tomatoes in the food processor just until combined in a coarse mixture scraping down the sides as necessary.

3. To assemble: Warm the pita on one side, directly on the grill or under the broiler, until slightly crisp but not brittle, about 1 minute. Lay a pita grilled side down on a 12-inch square of foil. Spread with a quarter of the tapenade, leaving a 1-inch border. Lay 4 basil leaves, followed by a quarter of the grilled vegetables, in a strip down the center. Roll the bread and foil together into a cone, using the foil as support and to seal the bottom. Complete the remaining wraps. Or, if you prefer, prepare all at once, assembly-line style. Peel down the foil as you eat.

MAKES 4 WRAPS

Substitutions
Try this with any leftover grilled or roasted vegetables.

Trim the Fat
This is a low-fat wrap if the olives are omitted and pita is not oiled.

Make Ahead/Take Away
The tapenade and vegetables may be prepared a day in advance, refrigerated, and used hot, reheated in the microwave for about 1 minute, or at room temperature. Assemble the wraps as described and serve immediately, warm or at room temperature.

Sweet Potato and Shiitake Mushroom Roll

 Sweet potatoes and woodsy shiitakes are one of my favorite vegetable combinations; they make a soul-satisfying vegetable wrap.

1 large sweet potato (about ¾ pound)
1 tablespoon unsalted butter
½ pound shiitake mushrooms, stems removed, caps sliced
¼ cup diced shallot
⅛ teaspoon dried thyme leaves
1 tablespoon flour
⅔ cup chicken or vegetable stock
2 tablespoons dry sherry
salt and freshly ground pepper to taste
2 large burrito-size flour tortillas
4 small escarole leaves, tough spines removed

1. Pierce the sweet potato several times with a fork and cook in the microwave on high until very tender, about 15 minutes. Cut in half lengthwise and, when cool enough to handle, peel and discard the skin.

2. While the sweet potato is cooking, melt the butter in a medium skillet over medium heat. Add the shiitakes, shallots, and thyme. Cook, stirring occasionally, until the mushrooms are wilted and the shallots are translucent, 5 to 7 minutes. Add the flour and continue stirring for an additional 1 to 2 minutes. Add the stock and sherry and cook, stirring frequently, until the sauce thickens and reduces to about ⅓ cup, about 3 to 5 minutes. Season with salt and pepper.

3. To assemble: Heat the tortillas, one at a time, directly on a gas flame, on a grill, or in a hot skillet, turning frequently, until hot and pliable, 5 to 15 seconds each. Or heat, stacked, in the microwave (see page 19). Smash half the sweet potato into the lower third of each tortilla. Salt lightly if you wish. Top each with half the escarole and mushroom sauce, making sure the ingredients don't quite touch the sides. Fold in the two sides and roll the wrap away from you. Cut in half on the bias.

MAKES 2 WRAPS

Substitutions

Use spinach or chard instead of escarole.

Trim the Fat

This is a low-fat wrap.

Make Ahead/Take Away

Sealed in wax paper, plastic wrap, or foil, and refrigerated, the wraps keep for up to a day. Reheat just until warmed through, either sealed in foil in a preheated 350°F oven for 10 to 15 minutes or in the microwave, unsealed, for about 1 minute. Serve warm.

Wild Mushroom Wrapture

 Grilled portobello mushrooms lend a deep, rich taste to this Mediterranean-inspired wrap. I used a standard 6-ounce package of sliced portobellos, found in most supermarkets, to make 2 wraps, but the recipe can easily be doubled. If you don't have cracked pepper, simply crack whole peppercorns with the bottom of a small heavy pot.

LEMONY CRACKED PEPPER VINAIGRETTE
1 small garlic clove, finely minced
½ teaspoon salt
¼ teaspoon coarsely cracked black pepper
1 tablespoon fresh lemon juice
2 tablespoons olive oil

1 6-ounce package sliced portobello mushrooms
1 small onion, cut into ½-inch slices
1 teaspoon fresh lemon juice
salt and freshly ground pepper to taste
2 pocketless pitas
olive oil for brushing pitas
2 tablespoons chèvre or Boursin cheese
1 small bunch of arugula, tough ends trimmed

1. To make the vinaigrette: Combine the garlic, salt, pepper, and lemon juice in a medium bowl. Whisk in the olive oil.
2. Add the mushrooms and onion and toss to coat well.
3. Heat an indoor or outdoor grill to medium-high or preheat the broiler. Grill or broil the vegetables, turning once or twice, until the mushrooms are soft and dark and the onions are well cooked, about 10 to 12 minutes total. (Reserve any marinade left in the bowl.) Return the vegetable mixture to the bowl, add 1 teaspoon lemon juice, any reserved marinade, and, if needed, additional salt and pepper and toss to combine.

4. To assemble: Brush one side of each pita with olive oil and grill, oiled side down, until hot and slightly crispy but not brittle, about 1 minute. Lay a pita on a 12-inch square of foil. Spread the soft side of each pita with 1 tablespoon cheese. Distribute half of the arugula and then half of the mushroom-onion mixture in a strip down the center. Roll the bread and foil together into a cone, using the foil as support and to seal the bottom. Peel down the foil as you eat.

MAKES 2 WRAPS

Trim the Fat
Reduce the fat by not brushing the pita with olive oil.

Make Ahead/Take Away
Best eaten warm or at room temperature, although leftover wraps eaten right out of the refrigerator for a midnight snack are also heavenly. Seal well in foil and refrigerate for up to 6 hours. Before eating, let sit at room temperature for up to 3 hours or reheat in a 350°F oven just until warm, for about 10 to 15 minutes.

Thai Noodle Veggie Wrap

 Cellophane noodles and crisp vegetables are wrapped in delicate rice paper and served with a sweet, hot peanut sauce for dipping. These make a terrific light lunch or appetizer, served on a bed of Bibb or green leaf lettuce. Both tamari, a type of soy sauce, and cellophane noodles can be found in the Asian section of the supermarket or in specialty stores. Fish sauce, another Asian ingredient, is becoming easier to find, although you may have some trouble in certain parts of the country. If unavailable, salt to taste instead.

1 cup smooth peanut butter
⅓ cup cider vinegar
3 tablespoons tamari
1 teaspoon to 1 tablespoon packed brown sugar, depending on
    sweetness of peanut butter
1½ teaspoons cayenne pepper or to taste

1 2-ounce bundle of cellophane noodles or bean threads
⅔ cup green beans (about 24), thinly sliced crosswise
4 carrots, peeled and shredded
½ cup coarsely chopped cilantro
¼ cup chopped roasted peanuts
4 scallions, both white and green parts, finely chopped
fish sauce or salt to taste
24 7-inch round rice paper wrappers

1. To make the peanut sauce: In a blender, combine the peanut butter, ¼ cup plus 1 teaspoon of the cider vinegar, tamari, brown sugar, cayenne pepper, and ¾ to 1 cup water, stopping and mixing with a spoon once or twice to combine and scrape down the sides. (All peanut butters are a different texture, so add just enough to make it dipping consistency.)

2. Pour boiling water over the cellophane noodles (or bean threads) in a medium bowl and allow to sit until they are soft, 3 to 5 minutes. Drain well and rinse with cold water. Drain again, shaking the colander to remove excess water. Toss with the beans, carrots, cilantro, peanuts, scallions, and fish sauce to taste.

3. To assemble: Immerse 2 or 3 rice paper sheets in a medium bowl filled with warm water. As soon as they are soft and pliable but not mushy (after about 1 minute), lay them out on a clean

absorbent kitchen cloth. (As you work, you may lose a few that tear; just discard them.) Place about a rounded tablespoon of the filling in the center of each. Fold up once from the bottom, just to cover the filling, then gently press the wrapper against the filling to compress and spread it a little. Fold in the sides and roll as tightly as possible without tearing the wrapper. (They will make rectangular wraps.) Repeat the procedure with the remaining ingredients, tossing the filling frequently to combine the vegetables and noodles. Serve with the dip.

MAKES 24 APPETIZER-SIZE WRAPS, SERVING 4 FOR LUNCH

Trim the Fat

Since all the fat is in the dip, go light when you dunk and you'll reduce the fat dramatically. Or, use the Vietnamese Summer Roll Dip on page 146.

Make Ahead/Take Away

Although not essential, these will hold together even better when sealed tightly in plastic wrap and refrigerated for about 30 minutes. (They'll hold for about 3 hours this way.) The dipping sauce can be prepared a day in advance and refrigerated. Serve cold or at room temperature.

Veggie Pizza Takes a Spin

 East meets west when a quick stir-fry fills a flatbread pizza. The resulting wrap is fresh tasting, light, and summery.

2 tablespoons olive oil
1 large onion, sliced
1 yellow or red bell pepper, cored, seeded, and cut into strips
1 cup small broccoli florets
4 garlic cloves, minced
salt and freshly ground pepper to taste
4 pocketless pitas
1 14-ounce can diced Italian-style tomatoes, well drained
4 ounces fresh mozzarella, coarsely grated or chopped
⅔ cup coarsely grated Parmesan cheese, such as Parmigiano-Reggiano
about 20 fresh basil leaves

1. Heat the oil in a wok over high heat. Add the onion and pepper and cook, stirring frequently, for about 2 minutes. Add the broccoli and garlic and continue to cook, stirring frequently, until the broccoli is bright green and tender-crisp, about 3 to 5 minutes. Season with salt and pepper. Turn off the heat.

2. To assemble: Preheat the broiler. Place each pita on a 12-inch square of foil on 1 large or 2 small baking sheets. Leaving a 1-inch border, top each pita with about a quarter of the tomatoes, mozzarella, and Parmesan. Broil open-faced, until the cheese bubbles, 3 to 5 minutes, cooking in 2 batches if you have a small broiler. Immediately top the center of each pita, in a strip down the middle, with about a quarter of the vegetables and basil. Wrap into a cone, folding the bread and foil together, using the foil as support and to seal the bottom. Peel down the foil as you eat.

MAKES 4 WRAPS

Shortcuts

To cut preparation time, purchase 3 to 4 cups precut salad bar vegetables of your choice to use instead of the onion, broccoli, and peppers. Cook them with the oil and garlic just until tender-crisp.

Make Ahead/Take Away

Best eaten immediately

6 bean and legume wraps

Bean and legumes snuggle comfortably into wraps like . . . well, like peas in a pod! In this chapter tortillas are filled with some classic combinations, like beans and salsa in the Chili Bean Wrap or curry and lentils in the fiery Vegetable-Lentil Vindaloo with Mango Raita. But there are plenty of unconventional mixes to whet your appetite as well, like the Miami Beach Black Bean Wrap, in which tortillas surround a savory bean-jícama filling.

For convenience and speed I use only canned or frozen beans in this book. Always drain and rinse canned beans before using and try a variety of brands until you find a favorite, because quality varies. I stock cans of my favorite beans— black, cannellini, and chickpeas—in the pantry for last-minute wraps. (Of course, when cooking with these recipes, feel free to swap your favorite beans for mine.)

Many people don't know that peanuts are technically legumes too. Peanut butter and dried legumes are also easy to keep on hand. Tempeh, the nutty-textured soybean product used in Who-Needs-Meat Fajitas with Ancho Chili Sauce, is found in the produce section of most supermarkets, next to the tofu. It is made from fermented soybeans and comes in a well-sealed package, so it keeps well in the refrigerator; just check the expiration date. (For a tofu recipe, see Steamed Vegetable Wrap Two Ways, page 72.)

Burritos are the granddad of many bean wraps, and some of these recipes, such as the Chili Bean Wrap, are really takes on the traditional burrito. So it seems appropriate to interject a note on improvising other quick weekday bean burrito wraps at home. Start with leftover or quickly boiled rice (page 14) and a mixture of any beans, seasoned to taste. Just briefly sauté onions and optional additions like garlic, minced jalapeños, diced poblano chilies or ground chilies, and cumin or whatever seasonings entice you. Add the drained, rinsed beans and simmer with stewed tomatoes or diced tomatoes or even stock, water, or salsa, if you wish. People add all kinds of things to the beans, from corn kernels and cubed winter squash to cinnamon and handfuls of fresh cilantro.

When assembling a bean or legume wrap, place the rice down first to prevent the tortilla from getting soggy, followed by the beans, shredded lettuce, and salsa. If you like, top it all off with traditional extras, like chopped avocado or guacamole, sour cream or shredded Monterey Jack or Cheddar. Then wrap it up! It'll be sloppy but good. As with all moist bean and legume wraps, you can lay down a piece of foil under the tortilla and wrap it with the bread, then peel down the foil as you eat. Or, if you'd like diners to have fun assembling their own burritos, serve the beans in a pot at the table, surrounded by accompaniments in bowls and tortillas in a cloth-lined basket (see Vicki's Vegetarian Texas Tacos, page 90).

Finally, the thing that delighted me most about bean and legume wraps in this chapter was how many were excellent served at room temperature or even cold and how well many of them reheated (see page 13).

BEAN AND LEGUME

Italian White Bean Burrito with Salsa Cruda

Who-Needs-Meat Fajitas with Ancho Chili Sauce

Vicki's Vegetarian Texas Tacos

Chili Bean Wrap

Miami Beach Black Bean Wrap

Crispy Twice-Baked Bean and Cheese Wrap

Mediterranean Wrap

Curried Couscous with Spinach and Chickpeas

Moroccan Cracked Wheat and Chickpea Roll-Up

Vegetable Hummus Lavash

Reggae Roll

Mess o' Greens and Beans

Vegetable-Lentil Vindaloo with Mango Raita

Italian White Bean Burrito with Salsa Cruda

 Even after testing (and consuming) dozens of wraps, the scrumptious simplicity of this burrito delighted me: Top tortillas with beans, garlic, and cheese and bake; add salsa and fresh basil; then wrap it up!

SALSA CRUDA
1 large ripe tomato, chopped
4 large green or black olives, pitted and chopped
2 tablespoons chopped shallot
2 teaspoons balsamic vinegar
salt and freshly ground pepper to taste

4 large burrito-size flour tortillas
1 19-ounce can cannellini (white kidney) beans, drained and rinsed
1 large garlic clove, minced
½ cup coarsely grated Asiago cheese
16 fresh basil leaves

1. Preheat the oven to 425°F. To make the Salsa Cruda: Combine the tomato, olives, shallot, vinegar, and a generous pinch of salt and pepper in a small bowl. Set aside.
2. Place the tortillas on 2 baking sheets. Toss together the beans, garlic, and cheese in a small bowl. Divide them equally among the tortillas and spread evenly, leaving a 2-inch border. Heat in the oven just long enough to melt the cheese, about 3 to 5 minutes.
3. To assemble: Working quickly, slide each burrito onto a piece of foil or kitchen towel. (This will protect your hands when rolling the hot wrap.) Divide the Salsa Cruda and basil equally over the beans.

Fold in the sides of the tortillas and roll. (If the tortillas are too brittle to fold, don't worry; just roll them without folding in the sides.) Eat immediately.
MAKES 4 WRAPS

Trim the Fat
To make this a low-fat burrito, reduce the amount of Asiago cheese to ⅓ cup.

Make Ahead/Take Away
The Salsa Cruda and bean mixture can be prepared the day before, chilled, then brought to room temperature and assembled as described. The wraps, however, are best eaten immediately, serve warm.

Who-Needs-Meat Fajitas with Ancho Chili Sauce

 Even the most ardent tofu hater, my husband, adored these hearty vegetarian fajitas. The secret is that they use tempeh, an Indonesian fermented soy product with a nutty texture. The tempeh absorbs plenty of ancho chili sauce. It can be found next to the tofu, in the produce section of your supermarket. Ancho chilies, which are dried poblanos, can be found in most supermarkets, often in the produce section.

1 ancho chili (3 to 4 inches long)
1 8-ounce package tempeh, thinly sliced
2 tablespoons fresh lime juice
1½ tablespoons vegetable oil
2 garlic cloves, minced
¾ teaspoon ground cumin
salt and freshly ground pepper to taste
1 large onion, sliced
1 large green bell pepper, cored, seeded, and cut into strips
2 plum tomatoes
4 large burrito-size flour tortillas
¼ cup sour cream
1 avocado, peeled, pitted, and diced
2 cups shredded romaine lettuce
⅓ cup mild salsa, homemade or store-bought

1. Bring a small pot of water to a boil. Add the ancho chili, reduce heat to a low simmer, and cook until the ancho is very soft, about 3 to 5 minutes. Drain. When cool enough to handle, remove the stem and seeds and add the flesh to a blender. Set aside.

2. Toss the tempeh with the lime juice, 1½ teaspoons of the oil, the garlic, cumin, and a pinch of salt and pepper. Set aside.

3. Heat the remaining oil in a large non-stick skillet over high heat. Add the onion, pepper, and tomatoes, and cook, stirring frequently, until the tomatoes start to soften but do not collapse, about 3 minutes. Add the tomatoes to the ancho in the blender. Continue cooking and stirring until the onion is soft and partly browned and the pepper is softened, 5 to 7 minutes longer.

4. Blend the ancho chili and cooked tomatoes with 2 tablespoons of water. Season with salt. Add the sauce to the skillet along with the marinated tempeh. Reduce the heat to medium and cook, shaking frequently to distribute the sauce. (Stirring breaks up the tempeh.) Cook until most, but not all, of the sauce is absorbed, about 5 minutes. Salt generously.

5. To assemble: Heat the tortillas, one at a time, directly on a gas flame, on a grill, or in a hot skillet, turning frequently, until hot and pliable, about 5 to 15 seconds each. Or heat, stacked, in the microwave (see page 19). Place a warm tortilla on a plate and spread with 1 tablespoon sour cream, leaving a 1-inch border. Distribute a quarter of the fajitas mixture in a thick horizontal strip across the bottom third of the tortilla, making sure the ingredients don't quite touch the edges. Fold in the two sides and roll the wrap away from you. Complete the wraps with the remaining ingredients. Or, if you prefer, prepare all at once, assembly-line style. Cut in half on the bias.

MAKES 4 WRAPS

Trim the Fat

This is a low-fat wrap if no oil is added to the tempeh marinade. In addition, add 1 teaspoon, instead of 1 tablespoon, oil to the pan. Finally, use 3 tablespoons sour cream (or use a low- or reduced-fat version) and eliminate the avocado.

Make Ahead/Take Away

The filling can be made a day or 2 ahead and stored in the refrigerator. Reheat the filling, covered, on high in the microwave until hot, about 2 to 3 minutes. Assemble the wraps as described. Serve immediately.

Vicki's Vegetarian Texas Tacos

 My friend Vicki is a Texas transplant to New England, where she likes to feature her fresh garden vegetables in every meal. This instant family dinner is open-ended. Just be sure to set out a variety of toppings on the table while the beans cook.

1 tablespoon vegetable oil
1 small onion, minced
2 garlic cloves, minced
4 teaspoons ground cumin
4 teaspoons chili powder
2 15.5-ounce cans black or pinto beans, drained and rinsed
½ cup medium or hot salsa
salt to taste
hot sauce to taste
⅓ cup grated Cheddar or Monterey Jack cheese
about 20 taco shells

TOPPINGS (CHOOSE 3 OR MORE PLUS SALSA)
salsa, store-bought or homemade
diced zucchini
shredded lettuce
cilantro leaves
diced avocado, tossed with a splash of lime juice
grated Cheddar cheese
sliced scallion or chopped onion
diced green, red, or yellow bell pepper
lime wedges

1. Preheat the oven to 350°F. Heat the oil in a large skillet over medium heat. Add the onion and garlic and cook, stirring occasionally, until the onion is translucent, about 5 minutes. Add the cumin and chili powder and stir until they are aromatic, about 1 to 2 minutes longer. Add the beans and salsa and mash so the mixture is chunky or fairly smooth, as you prefer, right in the skillet using a potato masher, adding water as necessary to create a soft texture. Season with salt and hot sauce.

2. Transfer the beans to a small, attractive ovenproof casserole or crock, top with the $\frac{1}{3}$ cup grated cheese, and bake, until hot and starting to brown, 15 to 20 minutes. About 5 minutes before the beans are done, add the taco shells to the oven on a baking sheet. Serve the beans in their baking dish and the shells in a cloth-lined basket with all the toppings. Let diners assemble their own bean tacos, with toppings, to taste.

MAKES 20 SMALL TACOS, SERVING 8

Trim the Fat

To make this a low-fat taco, reduce the oil to 2 teaspoons and use $\frac{1}{3}$ cup cheese to top the beans before baking or as a side topping, but not both.

Make Ahead/Take Away

You can make the beans up to 2 days before serving and store in the refrigerator. The toppings can be made several hours before and refrigerated as well. Reheat the beans in the oven right before eating, adding a little water if necessary, until piping hot. Then set out with the toppings and enjoy. This is a sit-down meal, not appropriate for take away. Make the wraps right before eating, since they tend to get soggy.

Chili Bean Wrap

 Leftover or quickly boiled rice (page 14), black beans, and smoky chilies form the basis of this hearty vegetarian wrap. It can be assembled in very little time and even reheated in the oven in foil or in the microwave in a covered bowl. This has a kick; if you want to tame its fire, eliminate one of the chilies. Chipotle chilies can be found in the Latin section of the supermarket and specialty stores. For improvising bean burritos, see the notes at the beginning of this chapter (page 85). Take-out burrito fans may also want to add shredded lettuce.

1 tablespoon vegetable oil
1 large onion, chopped
2 garlic cloves, minced
2 teaspoons ground cumin
1 15-ounce can black beans, drained and rinsed
2 canned chipotle chilies, chopped
1 teaspoon adobo sauce from the canned chilies
1/4 teaspoon salt
4 large burrito-size flour tortillas
1/3 cup sour cream
2 cups cooked rice
1/2 cup mild salsa
1/4 cup cilantro leaves

1. Heat the oil in a nonstick skillet over medium heat. Add the onion and cook, stirring occasionally, until translucent, about 5 minutes. Add the garlic and cumin, and cook for an additional minute, then stir in the black beans, chipotles, adobo sauce, and salt. Simmer to heat through, about 5 minutes. (Don't worry if the mixture appears a bit dry; it blends beautifully with the salsa.)
2. To assemble: Heat the tortillas, one at a time, directly on a gas flame, on a grill, or in a hot skillet, turning frequently, until hot and pliable, about 5 to 15 seconds each. Or heat, stacked, in the microwave (see page 19). Spread a tortilla with about 1 1/2 tablespoons sour cream. Lay 1/2 cup rice in a thick horizontal strip about a third of the way up from the bottom. Top with a quarter of the black beans, salsa, and cilantro leaves. Fold in the two sides and roll the wrap away from

you. Complete the wraps with the remaining ingredients. Or, if you prefer, prepare all at once, assembly-line style. **MAKES 4 WRAPS**

Substitutions

Use your favorite beans, such as pinto or kidney, instead of black beans. Try a variety of salsas.

Trim the Fat

To make this a low-fat wrap, use light sour cream.

Make Ahead/Take Away

Store sealed in foil and refrigerated for up to a day. Reheat just until warm in a pre-heated 350°F oven for 10 to 15 minutes or unseal and reheat in the microwave, just until warm, on high for about 1 minute. Serve warm.

Miami Beach Black Bean Wrap

 This is one of my favorites—black bean salsa topped with a crunchy jícama salad, then rolled into a refreshing summer meal. Try this no-cook wrap on a hot day with a cold beer.

1 19-ounce can black beans, drained and rinsed
½ cup salsa
2 tablespoons fresh lime juice
1 red bell pepper, cored, seeded, and diced
1 small jícama (¾ pound), peeled and diced
½ cup diced red onion
½ cup packed cilantro leaves
1 jalapeño pepper, seeded and minced
¼ teaspoon salt
4 large burrito-size flour tortillas
¼ cup sour cream

1. Briefly pulse the beans, salsa, and 1 tablespoon of the lime juice in a food processor, just until combined (but not smooth), about 7 times. Set aside.

2. Combine the pepper, jícama, onion, cilantro, jalapeño, and salt in a large bowl with the remaining tablespoon of lime juice. Toss to combine.

3. To assemble: Heat the tortillas, one at a time, directly on a gas flame, on a grill, or in a hot skillet, turning frequently, until hot and pliable, 5 to 15 seconds each. Or heat, stacked, in the microwave (see page 19). Lay a rounded third cup of the black bean salsa in a thick horizontal strip across the bottom third of the tortilla, making sure the ingredients don't quite touch the edges. Top with a quarter of the salad. Spread 1 tablespoon sour cream lightly over the top. Fold in the two sides and roll the wrap away from you. Complete the wraps with the remaining ingredients. Or, if you prefer, prepare all at once, assembly-line style. Cut in half on the bias.

MAKES 4 WRAPS

Trim the Fat
This is a low-fat wrap.

Make Ahead/Take Away
Make the black bean salsa and pepper-jícama salad up to a day before serving and refrigerate, but assemble the wraps right before eating. Serve cold or at room temperature.

Crispy Twice-Baked Bean and Cheese Wrap

 Just a few convenient ingredients add up to more than the sum of their parts—a crispy flatbread filled with melt-in-your mouth bean and Cheddar filling. This wrap calls for a cold glass of beer.

4 rounds of whole-wheat mountain bread
4 teaspoons grainy mustard
1 16-ounce can baked beans, well drained but not rinsed
4 ounces sharp Cheddar cheese, grated (about 1⅓ cups)
¼ cup diced Vidalia, red, or Spanish onion
4 handfuls of bitter greens, such as mustard or arugula, torn into bite-size pieces
vegetable oil for baking sheet

1. Preheat the oven to 425°F. To assemble: Heat the mountain bread rounds one at a time in a dry skillet, turning frequently, until hot and pliable, 15 to 20 seconds each. Spread each round with 1 teaspoon mustard. Top the bottom third of each round with about ⅓ cup drained baked beans and ⅓ cup cheese, 1 tablespoon onion, and a handful of greens. Fold in the sides and roll away from you.

2. To cook: Lightly oil a baking sheet and place in the oven for 5 minutes. Carefully place the wraps, seam side down, on the warm baking sheet. Turn when they are well browned and very crisp, after about 3 to 5 minutes. Continue browning on the other side for about an additional 3 to 5 minutes. Allow to sit for 5 minutes before serving.

MAKES 4 WRAPS

Trim the Fat

This is a low-fat wrap if only 1 cup of cheese is used and the baking sheet is sprayed with vegetable oil. Use widely available low-fat baked beans, but read the labels carefully, since nutritional counts vary from brand to brand.

Make Ahead/Take Away

The wrap may be assembled 1 hour before cooking, but is best eaten warm within 30 minutes after cooking.

Mediterranean Wrap

 Roasted fennel and leeks with white beans and sun-dried tomatoes make up this sophisticated wrap.

1 fennel bulb, root end and tough outer layer discarded, bulb sliced, fronds (green tops) reserved and chopped (up to ¼ cup)
1 large leek, root end and tough greens trimmed, rinsed, and cut lengthwise into ½-inch strips
8 garlic cloves, unpeeled
3½ tablespoons olive oil, preferably fruity
salt and freshly ground pepper to taste
1 15-ounce can cannellini (white kidney) beans, drained and rinsed
24 sun-dried tomato halves packed in olive oil, drained and each cut in half
3 tablespoons freshly grated Romano cheese
4 teaspoons fresh lemon juice
4 large burrito-style flour tortillas

1. Preheat the oven 425°F. Toss the fennel, leek, and garlic cloves in 1 tablespoon of the olive oil in a shallow baking pan. Add salt and a generous amount of pepper. Roast until soft and lightly browned, shaking the pan or turning the vegetables twice to prevent sticking, about 25 to 35 minutes. Remove.

2. When the vegetables are cool enough to handle, place them, except the garlic, in a large bowl. Peel or squeeze out the soft cooked garlic into the bowl, discarding the skins. Add the beans, sun-dried tomatoes, Romano cheese, lemon juice, reserved fennel tops, and remaining 2½ tablespoons olive oil. Toss to combine. Season with salt and pepper.

3. To assemble: Wrap the tortillas in foil and return to the oven to warm while the vegetables cool slightly for about 2 to 4 minutes. (Do not overheat, or the tortillas will become brittle.) Or heat the tortillas, one at a time, directly on a gas flame, on as grill, or in a hot skillet, turning frequently, until hot and pliable, 5 to 15 seconds each. Distribute a quarter of the filling in a thick horizontal strip across the bottom third of a tortilla, making sure the ingredients don't quite touch the edges. Fold in the two sides and roll the wrap away from you. Complete the wraps with the remaining ingredients. Or, if you prefer, prepare all at once, assembly-line style. Cut in half on the bias.
MAKES 4 WRAPS

Trim the Fat

To make this a low-fat wrap, reduce the olive oil to 1½ tablespoons and use dry-packed sun-dried tomatoes, plumped in boiling water, rather than those packed in oil. Coarsely chop the plumped tomatoes before adding them to the filling. To compensate for the lost moisture, toss the filling in 2 tablespoons chicken or vegetable stock.

Make Ahead/Take Away

Sealed in wax paper, foil, or plastic wrap and refrigerated, the wraps keep well for up to a day. To reheat, unseal, then heat very briefly in the microwave, just to take off the chill, about 1 minute. Serve warm or at room temperature.

Curried Couscous with Spinach and Chickpeas

 This vegetarian wrap plays with contrasting colors, tastes, and textures—yellow and green, hot and sweet, soft and crunchy.

¼ **cup chopped walnuts**
1 tablespoon unsalted butter
1 large onion, diced
2 teaspoons minced peeled fresh ginger
4 teaspoons curry powder, preferably Madras
1 garlic clove, minced
1 cup drained canned chickpeas, rinsed
¾ **cup couscous**
¾ **teaspoon salt**
4 lavash rectangles
¼ **cup Major Grey's chutney**
½ **cup plain low-fat yogurt**
20 large spinach leaves

1. Over medium heat, toast the walnuts in a large dry skillet, stirring frequently, until they start to smell aromatic, 2 to 4 minutes. Reserve the nuts.

2. Melt the butter in a large skillet over medium heat. Add the onion and ginger and cook, stirring frequently, for 3 minutes. Add the curry and garlic and continue to cook and stir until the garlic is aromatic but not browned, about 2 minutes more. Remove from the heat.

3. Stir in the chickpeas, couscous, salt, and 1 cup boiling water. Cover tightly with foil or a lid. When all the water is absorbed, after about 5 minutes, fluff the couscous with a fork and stir in the walnuts.

4. To assemble: Lay a lavash rectangle on top of a piece of wax paper or foil (this will help the wrap hold together better). With a short end facing you, using a tablespoon, spread about 1 tablespoon chutney and 2 tablespoons yogurt over the lavash (don't worry if it's not perfectly even). Cover with about 5 leaves of spinach. Pile the couscous in a thick horizontal strip across the bottom third, making sure the ingredients don't quite touch the sides. Wrap, curling the bread under with your fingers as you roll and being

careful not to wrap the wax paper or foil into the spiral. Complete the wraps with the remaining ingredients. Or, if you prefer, prepare all at once, assembly-line style. Cut in half on the bias.
MAKES 4 WRAPS

Substitutions
If you prefer, lettuce may be substituted for the spinach. Use warmed large burrito-size flour tortillas instead of the lavash. Fold in the sides before you roll.

Trim the Fat
This is a low-fat wrap.

Make Ahead/Take Away
This wrap is best eaten at room temperature. Store unrefrigerated, sealed in wax paper, foil, or plastic wrap, for up to 4 hours. If you are planning to wait that long before serving, spread an additional tablespoon of yogurt onto each lavash or tortilla and make the couscous with an additional 2 tablespoons water to prevent the wrap from drying out.

Moroccan Cracked Wheat and Chickpea Roll-Up

 Medium cracked wheat (also called *bulgur*) can be found in many supermarkets near the rice and in all health food stores.

1 large onion, quartered
1 green bell pepper, cored, seeded, and quartered
2 garlic cloves, coarsely chopped or sliced
2 tablespoons plus 1 teaspoon olive oil
1 teaspoon ground cumin
1 cup medium cracked wheat or bulgur
1 14-ounce can stewed tomatoes
½ teaspoon salt or more to taste
1 15-ounce can chickpeas, drained and rinsed
¼ cup fresh lemon juice
12 oil-cured black olives, pitted and halved
freshly ground pepper to taste
6 cups shredded romaine lettuce
4 lavash rectangles

1. Briefly pulse the onion, green pepper, and garlic in a food processor, until coarsely chopped.

2. Heat 1 tablespoon of the oil in a small pot over medium heat. Add the chopped mixture and the cumin, stirring occasionally, until the onion is translucent, about 5 minutes. Stir in the cracked wheat, tomatoes, salt, chickpeas, and ½ cup water. Bring to a boil and reduce to a low simmer. Cook, covered, until the liquid is absorbed but the bulgur is still moist, about 15 minutes. Remove from the heat and allow to sit, covered, for 15 minutes longer (the bulgur will continue to cook). The wrap can be assembled when the cracked wheat has cooled to room temperature, or the wheat may be chilled at this point for up to 3 days. When you are ready to assemble the wrap, stir in 2 tablespoons of the lemon juice and the olives. If you like, season with extra salt and pepper.

3. Toss the lettuce with the remaining 2 tablespoons of lemon juice and 4 teaspoons olive oil in a medium bowl. Season generously with salt and pepper, and toss again to blend.

4. To assemble: With a short end facing you, spread a lavash evenly with about a quarter of the cracked wheat (about $1\frac{1}{4}$ cups each), leaving a 1-inch border. Top each with a quarter of the salad. Roll tightly, compressing the salad as you go. Complete the wraps with the remaining ingredients. Or, if you prefer, prepare all at once, assembly-line style. Cut in half on the bias if desired.

MAKES 4 WRAPS

Substitutions

Use heated large burrito-size flour tortillas (see page 19) instead of lavash.

Make Ahead/Take Away

The filling for this wrap can be made up to 2 days in advance and is good served at room temperature or icy cold. If you want to store the assembled wrap, use large burrito-size flour tortillas instead of lavash and chill the wraps, sealed in wax paper or plastic wrap, for up to 6 hours before serving.

Vegetable Hummus Lavash

 This classic Middle Eastern combination makes a stunning meal-in-one wrap, with its crispy-fresh vegetables and garlicky bean spread. For a really quick version, use store-bought hummus and ready-made salad bar fixin's.

1 cup broccoli florets,
1 15-ounce can chickpeas, drained and rinsed
¼ cup tahini
¼ cup fresh lemon juice
2 garlic cloves, coarsely chopped
¾ teaspoon ground cumin, optional
3 lavash rectangles
2 small carrots, peeled and grated
2 ounces (approximately 18) snow peas
2 plum tomatoes, sliced

1. Place the broccoli in a shallow heat-proof bowl in the microwave with 1 table-spoon water. Cover with a plate and heat on high just until emerald green, about 1 minute. Set aside.

2. Blend the chickpeas, tahini, lemon juice, garlic, cumin, and ¼ cup water in a food processor until smooth, scraping down the sides if necessary.

3. To assemble: With a short end facing you, spread a scant ½ cup hummus in a thick strip about a third of the way up from the bottom of a lavash rectangle, leaving a 1-inch border. Layer the carrots, snow peas, tomatoes, and broccoli in a strip on top of the hummus. Roll away from you. Complete the wraps with the remaining ingredients. Or, if you prefer, prepare all at once, assembly-line style. Slice in half on the bias if desired.

MAKES 3 WRAPS

Substitutions

Use warmed large burrito-size flour tortillas (see page 19) instead of lavash. Use 5 cups of any vegetables and wrap them raw or steamed as appropriate.

Trim the Fat

This is a low-fat wrap.

Make Ahead/Take Away

The hummus and vegetables can be prepared a day ahead and refrigerated. Once the wraps are assembled, they will keep in the refrigerator, sealed in wax paper, foil, or plastic wrap, for 4 to 6 hours.

Reggae Roll

 No worries; this is a PBJ sandwich for grown-ups that replaces the traditional grape jelly with a homemade Jamaican banana chutney.

BANANA CHUTNEY
2 bananas, peeled and diced
1½ tablespoons raisins
1½ tablespoons fresh lime juice
1 teaspoon grated peeled fresh ginger
½ small jalapeño pepper, seeded and minced
½ teaspoon ground allspice

2 lavash rectangles
½ cup smooth peanut butter
¼ cup honey-roasted or regular peanuts
4 green leaf lettuce leaves

1. To make the Banana Chutney: Toss together the bananas, raisins, lime juice, ginger, jalapeño, and allspice in a medium bowl just until combined.

2. To assemble: With the short ends facing you, spread each lavash with a quarter of the peanut butter, leaving a 1-inch border. Sprinkle with the peanuts and Banana Chutney. Top with lettuce and roll. Cut in half on the bias.

MAKES 4 SMALL BUT FILLING WRAPS

Substitutions
Use heated large burrito-size flour tortillas (see page 19) instead of lavash.

Make Ahead/Take Away
Sealed in plastic, wax paper, or foil and refrigerated, these wraps keep well for up to a day.

Mess o' Greens and Beans

 According to an African-American southern tradition, if you eat some-thing containing black-eyed peas on New Year's Eve (or Day), it will bring you good luck. But this succulent wrap is great anytime of the year, especially for serious greens lovers. Count me in!

2 teaspoons vegetable oil
1 medium onion, diced
1 cup diced tasso or spiced ham (about 4½ ounces)
½ cup white rice
1 bunch of collard greens (about 1 pound), tough stems discarded,
    coarsely chopped (about 6 cups)
1 10-ounce box frozen black-eyed peas
1 cup chicken broth
2 tablespoons red wine vinegar
½ teaspoon salt
1 teaspoon Tabasco or other hot sauce, plus extra for serving
6 large burrito-size flour tortillas

1. Heat the oil in a 4-quart pot over medium heat. Add the onion and ham and cook, stirring occasionally, until the onion is softened, about 2 to 3 minutes. Stir in the rice just until coated with oil, then add the collard greens, black-eyed peas, and chicken broth. Bring the liquid to a boil, reduce to a low simmer, cover tightly, and simmer until the liquid is absorbed and the rice is cooked, about 20 minutes. Remove from the heat and stir in the vinegar. Season generously with salt and plenty of hot sauce.
2. To assemble: Heat the tortillas, one at a time, directly on a gas flame, on a grill, or in a hot skillet, turning frequently, until hot and pliable, about 5 to 15 sec-

onds each. Or heat, stacked, in the microwave (see page 19). Lay about a sixth of the filling in a thick horizontal strip across the bottom third of a tortilla, making sure the ingredients don't quite touch the edges. For a secure wrap, fold the bottom end of the tortilla up over the filling, fold in the two sides, and then roll the wrap away from you. Complete the wraps with the remaining ingredients. Or, if you prefer, prepare all at once, assembly-line style.
MAKES 6 WRAPS

Substitutions
Use kale instead of collards.

Trim the Fat

This is a low-fat wrap if low-fat spiced ham is used. Or ham may be omitted.

Make Ahead/Take Away

The greens and bean mixture can be made a day in advance and reheated in the microwave on high just until warmed through, about 3 to 5 minutes, although they will not retain their brightness. Serve the wraps immediately, warm or at room temperature.

Vegetable-Lentil Vindaloo with Mango Raita

 The secret to this wrap is to season the curried lentil-vegetable stew with as much heat—that is, cayenne pepper—as you can take, because once its spiciness hits the neutral rice and the cool, sweet mango raita, the flavors all balance together beautifully.

1 tablespoon unsalted butter or vegetable oil
1 medium onion, coarsely chopped
2 teaspoons minced peeled fresh ginger
4 teaspoons curry powder, preferably Madras
1 cup dried lentils
1 14.5-ounce can stewed tomatoes
salt and cayenne pepper to taste
2 cups small cauliflower florets (about ½ pound)
½ cup fresh or frozen peas
10 large burrito-size flour tortillas
5 cups cooked rice

MANGO RAITA
2 large mangoes, peeled, pitted, and diced
⅔ cup plain yogurt
½ cup coarsely chopped cilantro

1. Melt the butter in a medium pot over medium heat. Add the onion and ginger and cook, stirring occasionally, until the onion starts to brown, about 5 minutes. Add the curry and continue to cook, stirring constantly, until the spices are aromatic, about 1 minute. Stir in the lentils, stewed tomatoes with their juices, and 3 cups water. Bring to a boil, reduce to a simmer, and cook, covered, until the lentils are soft, about 45 minutes. Season generously with salt and lots of cayenne pepper. (If you are making this well in advance, season just before assembling the wrap or go lighter on the cayenne, since it heats up over time.)

2. While the lentils are cooking, make the raita: Combine the mangoes, yogurt, and cilantro in a small bowl.

3. When the lentils are cooked, stir in the cauliflower, cover, and cook over medium heat until the mixture is firm but tender, about 5 minutes. Stir in the peas and cook until they are warmed through, about 2 minutes. Turn off the heat.

4. To assemble: Heat the tortillas, one at a time, directly on a gas flame, on a grill, or in a hot skillet, turning frequently, until hot and pliable, about 5 to 15 seconds each. Or heat, stacked, in the microwave (see page 19). Lay a warm tortilla on a 12-inch sheet of foil. Layer the ingredients in a thick horizontal strip across the bottom third of the tortilla, using 1/2 cup of rice, a scant 1/2 cup of the stew, and a heaping tablespoon of raita, making sure the ingredients don't quite touch the edges. Fold in the two sides and roll the wrap away from you, being careful not to include the foil in the spiral. Complete the wraps with the remaining ingredients. Or, if you prefer, prepare all at once, assembly-line style.

MAKES 10 TORTILLAS

Substitutions
Any kind of vegetable, like carrots or sugar snaps, would be good in this dish. If you can't find mango, replace it with 4 to 5 ripe nectarines.

Trim the Fat
This is a low-fat wrap.

Shortcuts
Buy precut cauliflower florets and shelled peas.

Make Ahead/Take Away
Because of the lentils, this recipe takes a bit longer than most of the wraps in this book. But it can be completed through step 1 up to 3 days in advance and stored in the refrigerator. Then reheat the lentils in a pot over medium heat and proceed with the rest of the recipe. The wraps should be eaten as soon as they are assembled.

7 chicken (and more) wraps

My chicken cooking classes are always extremely popular. People eat plenty of chicken but often have a limited recipe repertoire, so they're eager for inspiration to escape their workaday chicken rut. The chicken wraps in this chapter do the trick, and the couple of turkey and duck options make it even more interesting.

Of course the nature of chicken makes my job easy. Chicken is famous for its chameleonlike qualities—add smoky chilies and it evokes New Mexico in Santa Fe Chicken Wrap; garlic and rosemary, Italy, in Tuscan Chicken with Roasted Pepper and Arugula; or curry and mango chutney, India, in Madras Double-Mango Chicken.

Tailor recipes further to your taste by swapping one cut of chicken for another. Even though the recipes in this chapter focus on white breast meat, most Americans' preference, you should eat your wrap the way you like it. Use boneless thighs if you prefer them, as I do, and simply cook them a tad longer.

Chicken's flexibility extends to the wide variety of cooking methods that flatter both its flavor and its texture. So feel free to replace one cooking technique for another, like broiling for grilling or sautéing.

The wide availability of quality rotisserie chicken means that some of these recipes, like Roasted Chicken with Chutney and Cheddar, wrap up with little or no cooking. So during busy weekdays, pick up a precooked bird and get two meals for one: Monday's rotisserie chicken, followed by Tuesday's (or Wednesday's) exotic wrap, using leftovers.

SIMPLE TIPS FOR COOKING PERFECT CHICKEN

Chicken needs to be cooked all the way through—but just. If you overcook it, especially breast meat, it dries out. If you are unsure of doneness, here are two tests.

1. Chicken is done when it feels like the tip of your nose, firm but with a slight bounce. If it is as hard as your kitchen counter, it is too late, so add extra sauce for moisture, and better luck next time. A few tries at this and you'll get it down pat.

2. Many of my students prefer to sneak a peek. Slice into the middle and look. The chicken should be just opaque; translucent flesh is uncooked. Remember, the chicken will cook a little more once it is off the heat, so don't overdo it!

CHICKEN (AND MORE)

Chicken Satay in Pita

Cuban Chicken, Rice, and Beans

Madras Double-Mango Chicken

Triple-Corn Chicken Taco with Pecans

Pesto Chicken Wrap with Sun-Dried Tomatoes

Santa Fe Chicken Wrap

Szechwan Ginger Chicken

Tuscan Chicken with Roasted Pepper and Arugula

Sicilian Chicken with Grilled Tomato Sauce

Garlic Chicken with Italian Green Sauce

Roasted Chicken with Chutney and Cheddar

Roll-Over Club Sandwich

Thanksgiving in a Roll

Smoked Turkey Lavash with Horseradish and Apples

Peking Duck Wrap

Chicken Satay in Pita

 Crunchy peanuts add zip to this Indonesian-style pita pocket. If you use a standard, as opposed to nonstick skillet, add an extra 2 teaspoons of vegetable oil.

4 boneless, skinless chicken breast halves
1 teaspoon vegetable oil
2 teaspoons curry powder
1 cup unsweetened canned coconut milk
½ cup chunky peanut butter, preferably superchunk, or ⅓ cup smooth
   and 2 tablespoons chopped peanuts
2 tablespoons soy sauce
2 tablespoons cider vinegar
cayenne pepper to taste
1 cucumber, peeled, halved lengthwise, seeded, and sliced
1 cup torn lettuce leaves, such as romaine or green leaf
2 large pita pockets, cut in half to make 4 pockets

1. Bring a small pot of lightly salted water to a boil. Add the chicken breasts. Reduce the heat to a low simmer, cover, and cook, until the chicken breasts are just cooked through, about 10 minutes. Remove from the water and, when they're cool enough to handle, shred the chicken.

2. Heat the oil and curry powder in a medium nonstick skillet over medium heat, stirring constantly, just until the curry smells aromatic, 30 to 60 seconds. Immediately, so the curry does not burn, whisk in the coconut milk. Stir in the peanut butter, soy sauce, vinegar, cayenne pepper, and 2 to 4 tablespoons water, as needed to create the sauce

(quantity depends on the brand of peanut butter). Whisk to combine and simmer to marry the flavors for about 1 to 2 minutes. Add the shredded chicken back to the skillet. Stir to combine, then immediately remove from the heat.

3. Open the pita pockets and divide the cucumber slices and ¼ cup of the lettuce leaves equally among them. Top each with some chicken satay and any remaining leaves of lettuce.

MAKES 4 WRAPS

Substitutions

Being a dark meat lover, I enjoy this dish with chicken thighs. Since they are a bit smaller, use 5 to 6.

Shortcuts

Eliminate step 1 by using leftover chicken. Use about ⅔ pound boneless white or dark meat.

Make Ahead/Take Away

The chicken satay may be made a day ahead and stored in the refrigerator. To take it along, pack the pita, vegetables, and cold chicken satay mixture separately. Reheat the chicken, covered, with a little water in a microwave just until warm, about 1 or 2 minutes on high. Then assemble the pita. Serve warm or at room temperature.

Cuban Chicken, Rice, and Beans

 When I lived in downtown Manhattan, I frequented a little hole-in-the-wall joint on 14th Street for take-out chicken, yellow rice, and black beans. (As I walked home, the smell of the food would drive me wild with hunger.) This quick wrap version grew out of my nostalgia for that tiny restaurant that was perpetually filled with Latinos. The wrap holds together beautifully and reheats well. If you like it hot, add your favorite chili pepper with the onions; if you're a garlic lover, throw in a few minced cloves as well.

1 tablespoon olive oil
1 large onion, chopped
1 small green bell pepper, cored, seeded, and diced
2 skinless, boneless chicken thighs, cut into strips
1 5-ounce package yellow rice mix with seasonings
¾ teaspoon ground cumin
2 plum tomatoes, chopped
1 cup drained and rinsed canned black beans
¼ cup chopped cilantro leaves
4 large burrito-size flour tortillas
4 slices of boiled or baked ham
hot sauce, optional

1. Heat the oil in a medium saucepan over medium heat. Add the onion and green pepper and cook, stirring occasionally, until the onion is translucent, about 5 minutes.

2. Add the chicken, rice, seasoning mix, cumin, and 1⅔ cups water and stir for 1 minute to combine. Bring to a boil, reduce to a low simmer, cover, and cook until the rice has absorbed all the liquid, about 15 to 20 minutes. Stir in the tomatoes, black beans, and cilantro. Allow to cool slightly, uncovered, about 10 minutes.

3. To assemble: Heat the tortillas, one at a time, directly on a gas flame, on a grill, or in a hot skillet, turning frequently, until hot and pliable, about 5 to 15 seconds each. Or heat, stacked, in the microwave (see page 19). Lay a ham slice in the center of one of the tortillas. Spread about a quarter of the rice mixture on the bottom half of the tortilla, leaving a 1½-inch border. Roll tightly away from you. Complete the wraps with the remaining ingredients. Or, if you prefer, prepare all at once, assembly-line style. Cut in half on the bias. Serve warm with hot sauce if desired.

MAKES 4 LARGE WRAPS

Substitutions
Replace the ham with cooked diced chorizo mixed into the rice.

Trim the Fat
This is a low-fat wrap if the ham is omitted. To replace the lost flavor, add a couple of minced garlic cloves and 1 seeded and minced jalapeño pepper with the onion.

Make Ahead/Take Away
Sealed in wax paper, plastic wrap, or foil and refrigerated, the wraps will keep for up to 2 days. Reheat just until warmed through, either sealed in foil in a preheated 350°F oven for 10 to 15 minutes or in the microwave, unsealed, for about 1 minute on high.

Madras Double-Mango Chicken

 Here is a light, low-fat chicken salad wrap that uses both fresh mango and bottled mango chutney, with an added jolt of hot sauce for punch. I like to cook the chicken in an inexpensive stove-top cast-iron grill (see page 15), but it can also be broiled, grilled, or sautéed in a lightly oiled skillet.

¾ **cup plain low-fat yogurt**
4 **teaspoons curry powder**
3 **boneless, skinless chicken breast halves, each sliced into 4 long
   strips**
salt to taste
1 **mango, peeled, pitted, and cubed**
4 **slices of red onion**
2 **teaspoons hot sauce or to taste**
4 **large burrito-size flour tortillas**
4 **teaspoons mango chutney**
8 **green leaf lettuce leaves**

1. Stir together ½ cup of the yogurt and the curry in a small bowl. Add the chicken breasts and stir again to combine. Marinate for 30 minutes at room temperature.

2. Preheat a lightly oiled stove-top grill over high heat or, if you are using an outdoor grill, let the charcoal cook down to gray ash. Grill the chicken breasts, turning once, until just cooked through, about 3 minutes on each side. Salt the chicken, then combine it with the remaining ¼ cup yogurt, mango, onion, and hot sauce in a medium bowl. Salt again if necessary.

3. To assemble: Heat the tortillas, one at a time, directly on a gas flame, on a grill, or in a hot skillet, turning frequently, just until warm and pliable, about 5 to 15 seconds each. Spread 1 teaspoon chutney evenly onto each tortilla. Top each with 2 lettuce leaves and a quarter of the chicken mixture, in a thick horizontal strip across the bottom third of the tortilla, making sure the ingredients don't touch the edges. Fold in both sides, then roll the wrap away from you. Complete the wraps with the remaining ingredients. Or, if you prefer, prepare all at once, assembly-line style. Cut in half on the bias.

MAKES 4 WRAPS

Trim the Fat
This is a low-fat wrap.

Shortcuts

Marinate the chicken for 10 minutes instead of 30.

Make Ahead/Take Away

Sealed in wax paper, plastic wrap, or foil and refrigerated, the wraps keep well for up to 4 hours. Serve cold or at room temperature.

Triple-Corn Chicken Taco with Pecans

 If you're a big corn fan, try this chicken dish—breaded in cornmeal, sautéed with corn-pecan relish, and rolled in a corn tortilla. It has a fantastic taste that lies somewhere between Southeastern and Southwestern, but it will be welcome on tables all across the country.

The pan-roasted pecans lend a spectacular flavor to the relish. To save time, purchase small bags of chopped pecans in the supermarket.

4 corn tortillas
cornmeal, preferably stone-ground, for coating chicken
1 large boneless, skinless chicken breast half, pounded to ½-inch thickness between sheets of wax paper
salt to taste
2 teaspoons corn or any vegetable oil
¼ cup chopped pecans
⅔ cup fresh or frozen corn kernels
¼ cup chopped plum tomatoes
½ teaspoon grainy mustard
1 to 2 teaspoons hot sauce, to taste

1. Wrap the tortillas to cover thoroughly in a kitchen towel. Place in the top part of a steamer over boiling water, and cover tightly. Let steam for 1 minute. Turn off the heat and leave covered, allowing the tortillas to steam until the recipe is ready to assemble. Alternatively, wet your hands and rub them over each tortilla. Heat a skillet over medium heat. Add all the tortillas, stacked together, to the skillet. Heat until they become hot and pliable, about 1 to 2 minutes, rotating them every few seconds with tongs.

2. Sprinkle cornmeal on a plate. Thor-oughly coat the chicken breast and season with salt.

3. Heat the oil in a medium nonstick skillet over medium heat. Add the chicken breast and pecans. Cook, turning the chicken once and stirring the nuts frequently to prevent burning, until the chicken is crisp on both sides and cooked through, about 3 minutes. Remove the chicken to a cutting board and cover loosely with foil.

4. Stir the corn, tomatoes, 2 tablespoons of water, and the mustard into the nuts in the skillet. Season with salt and hot sauce. Continue cooking, stirring frequently, to blend the flavors and cook the corn, about 2 minutes, adding another tablespoon of water if additional moisture is needed. Watch carefully that the nuts don't burn.

5. To assemble: Cut the chicken into 8 thin slices. Set out a basket of the warm tortillas alongside a small platter of the chicken with the relish, and tongs for rolling your own. Alternatively, preroll them, distributing 2 slices of chicken and a generous spoonful of corn-pecan relish in a strip down the center of each tortilla. Roll from left to right.

MAKES 4 SMALL WRAPS

Substitutions
Use turkey cutlets instead of chicken.

Make Ahead/Take Away
Serve immediately.

Pesto Chicken Wrap with Sun-Dried Tomatoes

 Pan-toasted walnuts add crunch, but the surprise ingredient here is couscous, which cooks almost instantly and absorbs some of the Mediterranean flavors. Use light or dark chicken meat, or a combination, in this wrap.

¼ teaspoon salt or more to taste
1 cup plain couscous
1 garlic clove, peeled
2 cups fresh basil leaves
3 tablespoons olive oil
⅛ teaspoon freshly ground pepper
½ cup grated Parmesan cheese
⅓ cup coarsely chopped walnuts
4 large burrito-size flour tortillas
12 ounces shredded cooked chicken (3 to 4 cups)
16 sun-dried tomato halves packed in oil, drained and coarsely chopped
1 yellow bell pepper, cored, seeded, and diced

1. Pour 1½ cups boiling water mixed with ⅛ teaspoon of the salt over the couscous in a small bowl. Cover well and set aside.

2. To make the pesto: Combine the garlic, basil, olive oil, remaining ⅛ teaspoon salt, and pepper in a blender. Blend well until smooth. Stir in the cheese.

3. Toast the walnuts in a small heavy dry skillet over medium heat, stirring constantly, until aromatic, watching closely to prevent burning, about 3 to 5 minutes. Set aside.

4. To assemble: Heat the tortillas, one at a time, directly on a gas flame, on a grill,

or in a hot skillet, turning frequently, until hot and pliable, about 5 to 15 seconds each. Or heat, stacked, in the microwave (see page 19). Distribute 2 tablespoons pesto, ½ scant cup couscous, ¾ to 1 cup chicken, and a quarter of the walnuts, sun-dried tomatoes, and peppers evenly over a tortilla, leaving a 1-inch border. Roll up into a wrap. Complete the wraps with the remaining ingredients. Or, if you prefer, prepare all at once, assembly-line style. Cut in half on the bias.

MAKES 4 WRAPS

Substitutions
Skip step 2 and use $\frac{1}{2}$ cup ready-made pesto, with the oil well drained. Replace tortillas with lavash rectangles.

Make Ahead/Take Away
Sealed in wax paper, plastic wrap, or foil and refrigerated, the wraps will keep for up to a day. If you plan to eat it cold, soak the couscous in 2 more tablespoons of water and add up to $\frac{1}{2}$ tablespoon extra pesto on each roll. Otherwise, reheat just until warmed through, sealed in foil in a preheated 350°F oven for 10 to 15 minutes or in the microwave, uncovered, for 1 minute on high. Serve warm.

Santa Fe Chicken Wrap

 This spicy wrap has a smoky flavor that comes from grilling the chicken and the vegetables and is reinforced with the flavor of chipotle peppers (which are smoked jalapeños that can be found in the Latin section of the supermarket). If you can't grill the chicken outside, grill it inside or broil it—the cooking time won't change.

¾ **cup plain low-fat yogurt**
3 canned chipotle chilies, minced
1 tablespoon fresh lime juice
½ **teaspoon salt**
2 boneless, skinless chicken breast halves, each sliced into 4 long
 strips
1 cup uncooked rice or 2 cups heated leftover cooked rice
1 poblano or Italian frying pepper, cored, seeded, and cut into 8 strips
4 scallions, trimmed
4 large burrito-size flour tortillas
1 large plum tomato, cut into thin wedges
4 teaspoons adobo sauce from the canned chipotle chilies
lime wedges

1. Thoroughly combine ½ cup of the yogurt, the chipotle chilies, lime juice, and salt in a small bowl. Add the chicken and stir to coat. Marinate at room temperature for 30 minutes. If using leftover rice, skip to step 3.

2. Bring about 2 quarts lightly salted water to a rapid boil. Add the rice and boil until it is cooked, about 18 minutes. (The rice may be cooked in advance and then reheated in the microwave.)

3. Preheat a lightly oiled stove-top grill or outdoor grill over medium-high heat. Grill the chicken breast, pepper strips, and scallions, turning once, just until the

chicken is cooked through, about 3 minutes on each side.

4. To assemble: Heat the tortillas, one at a time, directly on a gas flame, on a grill, or in a hot skillet, turning frequently, until hot and pliable, about 5 to 15 seconds each. Or heat, stacked, in the microwave (see page 19). Distribute ½ cup of rice, 2 strips of the grilled chicken, a quarter of the vegetables and tomato, 1 tablespoon of the remaining yogurt, and 1 teaspoon adobo sauce in a thick horizontal strip across the bottom third of the tortillas, making sure that the ingredients don't quite touch the edges. Fold in the two sides and roll the wrap away from you. Complete the wraps with the remaining ingredients. Or, if you prefer, prepare all at once, assembly-line style. Cut in half on the bias. Serve with lime wedges.

MAKES 4 WRAPS

Substitutions
Use 3 chicken thighs instead of the breasts. Use a broiler instead of a grill.

Trim the Fat
This is a low-fat wrap.

Shortcuts
Omit the marinating.

Make Ahead/Take Away
Sealed in wax paper, foil, or plastic wrap and refrigerated, the wraps will keep for up to 6 hours. Before eating, let sit at room temperature for 1 hour or reheat just until warmed through, either sealed in foil in a preheated 350°F oven for 10 to 15 minutes or in the microwave, unsealed, for about 1 minute on high. Serve warm or at room temperature.

chicken (and more) wraps 121

Szechwan Ginger Chicken

 Quick and easy: Szechwan and hoisin sauce can be purchased in the Asian section of your supermarket and they both keep well in the refrigerator.

1 tablespoon vegetable oil
3 slices peeled fresh ginger
4 scallions, white and green parts separated, trimmed, and cut into
    2-inch pieces
2 skinless, boneless chicken breast halves, cut into small cubes
1 small yellow bell pepper, cored, seeded, and cut into thin strips
1 tablespoon Szechwan sauce or hot sauce to taste
2 large burrito-size flour tortillas
2 tablespoons hoisin sauce
¼ cup finely chopped Napa or any kind of green cabbage
2 tablespoons cilantro leaves

1. Heat the oil, ginger, and scallion whites in a wok or large skillet over high heat. Add the chicken and pepper and cook, stirring constantly, until the chicken is white on the outside. Add the Szechwan sauce and stir just until the chicken is cooked, about 3 to 5 minutes. Remove the ginger.

2. To assemble: Heat the tortillas, one at a time, directly on a gas flame, on a grill, or in a hot skillet, turning frequently, until hot and pliable, about 5 to 15 seconds each. Or heat, stacked, in the microwave (see page 19). Spread each tortilla with 1 tablespoon hoisin sauce, leaving a 1-inch border. Distribute half of the chicken mixture, scallion greens, cabbage, and cilantro leaves in a thick horizontal strip across the bottom third of each tortilla, making sure the ingredients don't quite touch the edges. Fold in the two sides and roll the wraps away from you. Cut in half on the bias.
MAKES 2 WRAPS

Substitutions
Instead of chicken, try pork or shrimp.

Trim the Fat
This is a low-fat wrap.

Make Ahead/Take Away
Sealed in wax paper, foil, or plastic wrap and refrigerated, the wraps keep for up to 6 hours. Reheat just until warmed through, either sealed in foil in a preheated 350°F oven for 10 to 15 minutes or unsealed in the microwave for about 1 minute on high. Serve warm or at room temperature.

Tuscan Chicken with Roasted Pepper and Arugula

 Need to escape the workaday world? In only 15 minutes this recipe offers the flavors of an al fresco Italian meal eaten on a marble table beneath a grapevine-covered trellis.

As with all pocketless pita recipes, if you prefer not to roll it, you can serve the bread, focaccia-style, topped with the ingredients. When selecting jarred roasted peppers, try to find ones that appear fire-roasted and singed.

2 boneless, skinless chicken breast halves, cut into ½-inch strips
1 7-ounce jar roasted red peppers, drained and cut into 1-inch strips
2 tablespoons olive oil, preferably fruity
2 garlic cloves, minced
1 fresh rosemary sprig or 1 pinch dried
½ teaspoon salt
½ teaspoon freshly ground pepper
fresh lemon juice to taste
4 pocketless pita breads
1 bunch of arugula, tough ends trimmed

1. Preheat the oven to 425°F. Toss the chicken, roasted pepper, 1 tablespoon of the oil, the garlic, rosemary, salt, and pepper together in a small casserole or baking dish. Bake, uncovered, just until the chicken is cooked through, about 10 to 15 minutes. (Be careful not to over-cook.) Leave the oven on to warm the pita. Remove the rosemary and let the chicken mixture cool slightly. Season with lemon juice.

2. To assemble: Brush one side of each pita with the remaining tablespoon of olive oil. Heat them, oiled side down, directly on the oven racks until slightly crisp but not brittle, about 1 minute. Lay each pita on a 12-inch square of foil. Distribute a quarter of the chicken-pepper mixture and a quarter of the arugula in a thick strip down the center of each. Roll the bread and foil together into cones, using the foil as support and to seal the bottom.
MAKES 4 WRAPS

Trim the Fat
This is a low-fat wrap.

Make Ahead/Take Away
Serve immediately.

Sicilian Chicken with Grilled Tomato Sauce

 For the taste of summer any time of year, try this chicken wrap with smoky tomato sauce and a generous splash of your favorite hot sauce—mine is Cholula. If you don't own a grill, broil the chicken and vegetables.

3 boneless, skinless chicken thighs
3 large plum tomatoes, halved
1 large red bell pepper, cored, seeded, and cut into strips
1 medium onion, thickly sliced
3 garlic cloves, minced
2 tablespoons olive oil
salt and hot sauce to taste
¾ cup plain couscous
4 large burrito-size flour tortillas
about 20 large fresh basil leaves

1. Toss the chicken, tomatoes, pepper, onion, garlic, and oil in a large bowl. Marinate for 10 to 30 minutes at room temperature. Heat an indoor or outdoor grill to medium-high and grill the chicken and vegetables, turning frequently and pulling them off with tongs to a large bowl when cooked, after about 3 to 5 minutes for the tomatoes and 10 to 15 minutes for everything else. When cool enough to handle, shred or cut each chicken thigh into 5 or 6 pieces.

2. To make the sauce: Combine the tomatoes, 2 or 3 grilled onion slices, and 1 grilled pepper strip in the blender. Blend until smooth. Add salt and a generous amount of hot sauce. Toss with the grilled chicken and vegetables.

3. Boil 1 cup salted water in a small pot. Add the couscous, remove from heat, cover, and set aside until all the water is absorbed, about 5 minutes. Fluff the couscous with a fork.

4. To assemble: Heat the tortillas, one at a time, directly on a grill, on a gas flame, or in a hot skillet, turning frequently, until hot and pliable, about 5 to 15 seconds each. Or heat, stacked, in the microwave (see page 19). Distribute a rounded ⅓ cup couscous, a quarter of the grilled chicken, vegetables, and sauce, and 5 basil leaves in a thick horizontal strip across the bottom third of a tortilla, making sure the ingredients don't quite touch the edges. Fold in the two sides and roll the wrap away from you. Complete the wraps with the remaining ingredients. Or, if you prefer, prepare all at once, assembly-line style. Cut in half on the bias.

MAKES 4 WRAPS

Trim the Fat
This is a low-fat wrap.

Make Ahead/Take Away
In step 1, marinate without the tomatoes in the refrigerator for up to 24 hours. When ready to eat, toss with the tomatoes and grill. Or grill the chicken and vegetables up to a day ahead and store together in the refrigerator. When you are ready to eat, reheat the chicken briefly in the microwave, just until warmed through, 2 to 3 minutes on high, then assemble the wraps. Serve warm or at room temperature.

Garlic Chicken with Italian Green Sauce

 I was happily surprised by how easy it was to prepare this rustic roll: Toss the chicken in the oven, blend up a green sauce, and roll it all in a warm pocketless pita. (Don't fuss too much with the parsley; a few stems won't matter.)

3 boneless, skinless chicken breast halves, cut into strips
3 garlic cloves, minced
3 tablespoons olive oil, preferably fruity
large tomato, halved, seeded with a spoon, and sliced
salt and freshly ground pepper to taste
1 cup fresh parsley leaves
1½ tablespoons fresh lemon juice
1 tablespoon drained capers
½ teaspoon anchovy paste
4 pocketless pitas
1 yellow bell pepper, cored, seeded, and cut into strips

1. Preheat the oven to 425°F. Toss the chicken, garlic, and 1 tablespoon of the olive oil in a small baking dish. Add the tomato, salt, and pepper and stir to combine. Roast, uncovered, turning once, until the chicken is just cooked through, about 12 to 16 minutes. (Leave the oven on for the pitas.)

2. Prepare the sauce while the chicken is cooking. In a blender (not a food processor), blend the parsley, lemon juice, capers, anchovy paste, and remaining 2 tablespoons olive oil to combine. When the chicken is finished, let the dish cool slightly, then carefully tip the baking dish, leaving the ingredients inside but draining most of the liquid into the blender with the other ingredients. Blend until smooth.

3. To assemble: Place the pitas directly on the oven rack and bake until hot and just slightly crisp but still pliable, about 3 to 5 minutes. Lay the pita rounds on top of 4 12-inch squares of foil. Top each pita, in a strip down the center, with a quarter of the chicken mixture, green sauce, and yellow pepper strips, with the pepper spears sticking out over the top edge. Roll the bread and foil together into a cone, using the foil as support and to seal the bottom.

MAKES 4 WRAPS

Trim the Fat
This is a low-fat wrap if 1 tablespoon of olive oil is eliminated and replaced with 1 tablespoon water or chicken stock.

Make Ahead/Take Away
Best eaten immediately.

Roasted Chicken with Chutney and Cheddar

 I used roasted drumsticks for this roll, but you can roast 2 large chicken breast halves instead. Or, for an even easier wrap, omit the curry powder and use 1 cup leftover cooked chicken or turkey with a pinch of cayenne pepper.

6 chicken legs
2 teaspoons curry powder
salt to taste
2 tablespoons Major Grey's chutney
2 tablespoons plain yogurt or mayonnaise
2 lavash rectangles
hot sauce to taste
1 cup grated Cheddar cheese
4 large green leaf lettuce leaves

1. Preheat the oven to 425°F. Sprinkle the chicken legs with the curry powder, rubbing it under the skin. Roast the legs in a small baking pan until cooked through, about 25 minutes. When cool enough to handle, remove the meat from the bones, discarding the tendons and, if desired, the skin. Shred the chicken and add the salt.

2. To assemble: Spread half the chutney and half the yogurt on each lavash (don't worry if it isn't perfectly even), then splash generously with hot sauce. With a short end facing you, lay half the cheese, half the chicken, and half the lettuce horizontally in a strip across the bottom third of the lavash, making sure the ingredients don't quite touch the edges. Roll the wrap away from you. Cut in half on the bias if desired.
MAKES 2 WRAPS

Substitutions
Use a large burrito-size flour tortilla instead of the lavash.

Trim the Fat
To reduce the fat, cut cheese in half (or use a low- or reduced-fat version). Use nonfat yogurt, adding an extra tablespoon for moisture.

Make Ahead/Take Away
The legs can be roasted a day ahead and kept in the refrigerator. Sealed in wax paper, foil, or plastic wrap and refrigerated, the wraps will keep for up to a day. Serve at room temperature or cold.

Roll-Over Club Sandwich

 Occasionally I crave a club sandwich and order it at my local diner, but I'm always let down by the prefab sliced turkey and boring bread. This over-stuffed club uses real roasted turkey breast, spiked with roasted garlic mayonnaise, rolled with the usual accompaniments in a whole-wheat mountain bread—a new classic!

4 strips of bacon
4 thin scallops of turkey breast, about ¾ pound
7 garlic cloves, unpeeled
2 tablespoons mayonnaise
salt and freshly ground pepper to taste
2 rounds of whole-wheat mountain bread
2 to 4 romaine lettuce leaves, torn in half
2 slices of tomato, cut in half
2 slices of red onion, broken into rings

1. Preheat the oven to 425°F. Lay the bacon in strips on a baking sheet. Top with the turkey scallops and sprinkle with the garlic cloves. Roast for 5 minutes and turn the turkey. Continue roasting, until the turkey is just cooked through, about 5 to 10 minutes longer. Remove the turkey with tongs, set aside, and continue cooking the bacon and garlic until the bacon is crisp and the garlic is quite soft, about 5 to 10 minutes longer. Set aside.

2. Remove the garlic and, when it is cool enough to handle, peel the cloves or squeeze them out of their skins into a large bowl. Mash with a fork, add the mayonnaise, and stir to combine. Shred the turkey, crumble the bacon, and add to the bowl. Toss well with salt and pepper.

3. To assemble: Heat the mountain bread rounds, one at a time, in a hot skillet just until warm and pliable, 15 to 20 seconds each. Or heat, stacked, in the microwave (see page 19). Layer half the turkey mixture on each warm round, followed by half the tomato and half the red onion in a thick horizontal strip across the bottom third of the round, making sure the ingredients don't quite touch the edges. Roll away from you. Cut in half on the bias.
MAKES 2 WRAPS

Substitutions
Use chicken instead of turkey. Replace mountain bread rounds with taco-size flour tortillas.

Shortcuts

Use leftover chicken or turkey and thin strips of ham from the deli in place of the bacon. Skip the garlic if you're not turning the oven on.

Make Ahead/Take Away

Sealed in wax paper, foil, or plastic wrap and refrigerated, these wraps keep well for up to a day. Serve warm right after preparing or, if storing, remove from the refrigerator 15 minutes before serving.

Thanksgiving in a Roll

 I always make a gigantic turkey for Thanksgiving with large batches of side dishes, because leftovers taste even better than the main event for the cook, who gets to enjoy the food in a more relaxed manner. This wrap uses the classic Thanksgiving leftovers you'll probably have on hand, but feel free to improvise with your refrigerator pickings, substituting corn bread for bread stuffing or adding anything from pureed yams to brussels sprouts. If all the cranberry sauce is gone, don't despair. Try Major Grey's mango chutney instead; it's delicious.

Of course you don't have to limit yourself to enjoying this wrap once a year. Try it year-round using a quick sauté of turkey or even chicken cutlets (or store-bought rotisserie chicken), fresh or canned cranberry sauce, and packaged stuffing. For a lightning-quick gravy, see the note at the end of the recipe.

1⅓ cups cooked bread stuffing
2 cups shredded cooked turkey
¼ cup gravy
4 large burrito-size flour tortillas
¼ cup cranberry sauce
salt and freshly ground pepper to taste

To assemble: Heat the stuffing, turkey, and gravy on high in the microwave just until hot. You can heat the ingredients all at once or in batches, depending on the size of your microwave (cooking times will vary depending on how you decide to do this). Heat the tortillas, one at a time, directly on a gas flame, on a grill, or in a hot skillet, turning frequently, until hot and pliable, about 5 to 15 seconds each. Or heat, stacked, in the microwave (see page 19). Layer about ⅓ cup stuffing, ½ cup turkey, 1 tablespoon gravy, 1 tablespoon cranberry sauce (using a spoon to spread the sauce if necessary),

and salt and pepper in a thick horizontal strip across the bottom third of a tortilla, making sure the ingredients don't quite touch the edges. Fold in the two sides and roll the wrap away from you. Complete the wraps with the remaining ingredients. Or, if you prefer, prepare all at once, assembly-line style. Cut in half on the bias.

To assemble this wrap cold: Use lavash instead of tortillas, substitute ¼ cup mayonnaise for the gravy, and add ¼ bunch watercress leaves for each wrap. Spread each lavash with 1 tablespoon mayonnaise and then scatter evenly over each lavash a quarter of the turkey, cranberry sauce, watercress, and sprinkle with salt and pepper, making sure the ingredients don't quite touch the edges. Roll the wraps away from you. Cut in half on the bias.

MAKES 4 WRAPS

NOTE: QUICK GRAVY
1 tablespoon unsalted butter
1 tablespoon flour
½ cup chicken stock
salt to taste

Melt the butter in a small skillet or saucepan. Add the flour and cook over medium-low heat, stirring frequently, until the mixture is nut brown, about 2 to 3 minutes. Pour in the stock, whisking constantly, until it has thickened, about 2 minutes. Salt to taste if using homemade stock.

Remember that stuffing can be quite fatty, but if it isn't cooked in the turkey, a very low-fat version is a snap to assemble, using either homemade or packaged stuffing. Many packaged brands offer directions for low-fat versions of their mixes.

Trim the Fat

This is a low-fat wrap if you are careful about adding no or little fat to the stuffing and cooking it outside the turkey. In addition, for the hot wrap, eliminate the gravy and add more cranberry sauce to taste. For the cold wrap, omit the mayonnaise and add more cranberry sauce.

Make Ahead/Take Away

These sturdy wraps can be made up to a day in advance, then sealed in wax paper, foil, or plastic wrap and refrigerated. Reheat the wraps just until warmed through, either sealed in foil in a preheated 350°F oven for 10 to 15 minutes or unsealed in the microwave for about 1 minute on high. Or serve wraps cold, right out of the refrigerator.

Smoked Turkey Lavash with Horseradish and Apples

 This light but flavorful wrap is assembled in a flash. You can buy smoked turkey in the deli section of your supermarket.

⅔ cup plain low-fat yogurt
1½ to 2 tablespoons drained bottled horseradish, to taste
4 lavash squares
8 large red leaf lettuce leaves
1 pound sliced smoked turkey
1 firm apple, like Granny Smith or Cortland, cored and sliced into very thin wedges

1. Stir together the yogurt and horseradish in a small bowl.

2. To assemble: Spread a lavash evenly with about 1 heaping tablespoon of the horseradish mixture. Cover with 2 lettuce leaves and a quarter of the turkey, making sure the ingredients don't quite touch the edges. Spread the remaining heaping tablespoon of the horseradish mixture over the top, followed by a quarter of the apples. Roll away from you. Complete the wraps with the remaining ingredients. Or, if you prefer, prepare all at once, assembly-line style. Cut in half on the bias.
MAKES 4 WRAPS

Substitutions
Use large burrito-size tortillas instead of lavash. Trim the ends.

Trim the Fat
This is a low-fat wrap.

Make Ahead/Take Away
Sealed in wax paper or foil and refrigerated, the wraps keep for up to a day. Serve cold or at room temperature.

Peking Duck Wrap

 I love the deep flavor of duck. And now that boneless breasts are easy to find, it takes little effort to prepare quick duck dinners at home. To make the presentation special, follow the instructions for tying the wraps with scallions.

1 whole boneless duck breast with skin (about 1 pound)
1 tablespoon dry sherry
4 long scallions for tying wraps, root ends trimmed, optional
4 small taco-size flour tortillas
¼ cup hoisin sauce
4 medium Napa cabbage leaves
½ cup julienne jícama (about ¼ small jícama, peeled)
1 scallion, both white and green parts, chopped

1. With a sharp knife, cut the duck breast in half and score the skin, cutting several crosshatch marks to allow the fat to drain off. Sprinkle the sherry over the duck and let marinate for 20 minutes.

2. Meanwhile, preheat the oven to 425°F. Fill a large bowl with cold water if you are tying the wraps up. Bring a medium pot of water to a rolling boil and plunge the 4 long scallions into the water. Immediately drain them and put them into the cold water. Drain again and set aside for tying.

3. Roast the duck in a shallow roasting pan, skin side down, until medium-rare, about 15 minutes. Remove from the oven and allow to sit, skin side up, for 5 minutes. Slice into thin strips lengthwise with the skin on.

4. To assemble: While the duck is sitting, stack the tortillas and wrap in foil. Heat in the oven until hot and pliable, about 3 to 5 minutes. (Do not overheat or they will become brittle.) Or heat the tortillas, one at a time, directly on a gas flame, a grill, or in a hot skillet, turning frequently, until hot and pliable, about 5 to 15 seconds each. Working quickly, spread 1 tablespoon hoisin sauce on each warm tortilla, leaving a 1-inch border. Top each with a leaf of cabbage (frilly end sticking out over the top), a quarter of the duck, jícama, and chopped scallion, in a thick strip down the center. Roll from left to right, then, if you like, tie the center with a scallion, removing a layer of green scallion skin first if it's too thick.

MAKES 4 SMALL WRAPS

Make Ahead/Take Away
You may hold these wraps in a 250°F oven for 10 minutes.

8 fish and seafood wraps

Fresh fish and seafood are available everywhere, even in quality supermarkets. They work swimmingly in wraps, especially when folded into spicy sauces or cool, tangy dressings.

Fish like tuna, swordfish, and salmon are particularly tasty in wraps, where their bold taste seizes center stage even when accompanied by robust flavors, like kale and horseradish in the succulent Teriyaki-Glazed Salmon Spirals. Also, the ever-popular shrimp, with its sweet flavor and springy texture, contrasts perfectly with soft tortillas and assertive sauces.

Feel free to swap similar types of fish and seafood. Substitute oily fish, such as salmon, swordfish, or tuna, for each other. Or, when using seafood, exchange shrimp, scallops, crab, or lobster. Base your choices on personal taste and, most of all, freshness.

Freshness is of prime importance with fish and seafood, so try to cook it the same day you buy it (or, at most, a day later). Surprisingly, once cooked, many of these wraps hold quite well for 3 hours to a day.

Both fish and seafood cooks quickly. The key to great flavor and moist texture is not to overcook it. Further, any acid in the wrap ingredients, like lemon juice or vinegar, will continue to "cook" the fish. So, it is better to under- than overdo it; tuna should be a bit pink or red in the center; salmon and even scallops can be left a tad uncooked in the middle, as you prefer and all other fish and seafood should be heated just until cooked through. In fact, some of the shrimp recipes call for undercooking, such as the summery Mexican Shrimp Wrap with Two Salsas, because the shrimp continues to cook after it leaves the heat. Preparing shrimp yourself gives you an edge in ensuring it's been cooked properly, because sometimes store-bought cooked shrimp can be tough. But, in a pinch, take a shortcut and buy precooked shrimp—or, for a splurge, substitute cooked lobster.

For safety, keep raw fish in the refrigerator until ready to use and, once cooked, eat wraps immediately or chill. Leaving fish out at room temperature may allow bacteria to grow; in any case, cold is always the best way to preserve seafood's flavor and texture.

FISH AND SEAFOOD

California Wrap and Roll

Crab-Avocado Quesadilla with Cilantro Pesto

Deer Isle Lobster Roll with Roasted Corn Relish

Jambalaya Wrap

Mexican Shrimp Wrap with Two Salsas

Vietnamese Summer Rolls with Jícama Slaw

Savory Shrimp and Feta with Fennel Confit

Zydeco Shrimp

Pepper-Seared Scallops with Oranges

Scallop Vegetable Stir-Fry with Black Bean Sauce

Panfried Catfish Tacos with Cool Cabbage Slaw

Provençal Wrap

Roasted Salmon-Asparagus Roll

Teriyaki-Glazed Salmon Spirals

Wasabi-Steamed Salmon and Cabbage Bundles

New York Brunch Wrap

Seared Tuna Amandine

California Wrap and Roll

 California rolls, sushi with crab and avocado, have become a popular eat-out item. But making them at home requires a bit of skill and patience. This easy-to-assemble variation makes terrific do-ahead lunch or appetizers. Versatile lavash flatbread is effortless to wrap. Pickled ginger adds a zing and can be purchased in the Asian section of most supermarkets or in specialty stores.

1 cup white rice (not converted or 5-minute)
1 teaspoon salt
3 tablespoons rice wine vinegar
2 scallions, both white and green parts, trimmed and chopped
1¼ teaspoons drained bottled horseradish
2 teaspoons fresh lime juice
1 teaspoon soy sauce
1 small ripe avocado, preferably Hass, peeled, pitted, and sliced
2 lavash rectangles, cut in half
6 ounces sea legs (surimi) or crabmeat, picked over for cartilage
14 to 16 thin slices of pickled ginger

1. Boil 2 cups of water in a medium saucepan. Add the rice and salt and return to a boil, stirring once or twice. Reduce the heat to low and simmer, covered, stirring twice to promote stickiness, until all the moisture is absorbed, about 18 minutes. Allow to cool, uncovered, for about 15 minutes, or remove to a plate to speed cooling.

2. Combine the vinegar, scallions, horseradish, 1½ teaspoons of the lime juice, and the soy sauce in a small bowl. Stir into the rice. Toss the avocado and remaining ½ teaspoon lime juice together in a separate small bowl.

3. To assemble: With a long end of a lavash half facing you, lay a quarter of the rice mixture evenly over the lavash, leaving a 1-inch border. Distribute a quarter of the crab, avocado, and ginger slices evenly over the rice and roll away from you, as tightly as possible. Complete the wraps with the remaining ingredients. Or, if you prefer, prepare all at once assembly-line style. Slice in half on the bias if serving for lunch. For appetizers, cut into 1- to 2-inch pieces and serve with the spirals facing up.

MAKES 4 WRAPS SERVING 4 AS LUNCH OR ABOUT 10 AS AN APPETIZER

Substitutions

Instead of crab, try cooked lobster, shrimp, or scallops. Substitute warmed large burrito-size flour tortillas (see page 19) for the lavash. After they are rolled, cut off the ends. If you like, add strips of the traditional nori, the flat sheets of seaweed found in Asian specialty and health food stores, to the rice. Nori adds a by-the-sea briny taste to these rolls. Although it is costly, a little goes a long way and it keeps well.

Trim the Fat

This is a low-fat wrap if only half the avocado is used.

Make Ahead/Take Away

The rice can be made a day or two ahead, stored in the refrigerator, then reheated briefly in the microwave, just to take the chill off. Once assembled and sealed in wax paper, plastic wrap, or foil and refrigerated, the wraps keep for up to 4 hours. These wraps slice better for appetizers if they are made 1 to 3 hours ahead and then chilled. Serve cold or cool (out of the refrigerator for under 30 minutes).

Crab-Avocado Quesadilla with Cilantro Pesto

 For great appetizers, just cut each of the quesadillas into 3 or 4 triangles and serve with lime wedges. It is easy to improvise a wide variety of quesadilla combinations on your own; just don't fill them too full, and include some kind of cheese so they hold together well. I like to whip up quesadillas for quick weeknight meals—ham and cheese with pickled jalapeños; avocado, bean, and Jack cheese with salsa and lime; or simply the best household leftovers with any flavorful cheese.

1 large garlic clove
1 jalapeño pepper, seeded and cut into quarters
1 4-ounce can chopped mild green chilies, drained and rinsed
½ cup pecan halves
1 large bunch of cilantro, roots and tough stems removed (3 to 4 cups loosely packed)
¼ cup vegetable oil, plus about 2 teaspoons for skillet
8 to 9 small taco-size flour tortillas
2 cups coarsely grated Monterey Jack cheese
10 ounces crabmeat, picked over for cartilage
1 small ripe avocado, preferably Hass, peeled, pitted, and diced
1 lime, cut into wedges

1. Preheat a platter in a 200°F oven. Blend the garlic, jalapeño, mild chilies, pecans, cilantro, and ¼ cup oil in a food processor or blender, scraping down the sides as necessary, until well combined but not totally smooth.

2. To assemble: Spread about 1 rounded tablespoon of the cilantro pesto on each tortilla, leaving about a 1-inch border. Equally divide the cheese, crab, and avocado among the tortillas. Fold each in half.

3. To cook: Heat about ½ teaspoon (or you can brush it on) oil in a large nonstick skillet over medium heat. Cook 2 quesadillas at a time (if you don't have a large enough skillet, use a medium skillet and cook 1 at a time), turning when they are lightly browned and the cheese has started to melt, about 4 minutes total. Transfer to the oven platter and continue cooking until they are all done, adding oil for each batch. (The cheese will continue to melt in the oven.) Serve as is or cut into 3 to 4 triangles each and serve with lime wedges.

MAKES 8 TO 9 WRAPS, 24 TO 36 APPETIZERS

Substitutions

Instead of crab, use chopped cooked shrimp or lobster. In a pinch, use canned crabmeat.

Make Ahead/Take Away

These can be assembled 1 day before they are cooked. Once cooked, serve immediately.

Deer Isle Lobster Roll
with Roasted Corn Relish

 The magical pairing of lobster with roasted corn and corn tortillas makes for a pretty, upscale version of the traditional New England sandwich (lobster and mayonnaise on a crisped hot dog bun). I like to imagine enjoying this summery wrap on the veranda, overlooking the stunning rock and water inlets of Deer Isle.

4 corn tortillas
1½ teaspoons corn or vegetable oil
kernels from 1 ear of corn, about ¾ cup
½ cup finely diced red onion
½ small poblano pepper, cored, seeded, and finely diced (about ¼ cup)
1 small plum tomato, seeded and finely chopped
salt and freshly ground pepper to taste
½ pound cooked lobster meat, coarsely chopped or shredded
2 tablespoons mayonnaise
1 teaspoon fresh lime juice
4 handfuls of green leaf lettuce, torn into bite-size pieces

1. Wrap the tortillas well in a kitchen towel. Set in a steamer above boiling water. Cover well and steam for 1 minute, then turn off the heat and let sit, covered, until warm and pliable, about 15 minutes. (These will stay warm for a while, so don't worry too much about timing.) Alternatively, wet your hands and rub them across each tortilla. Heat a skillet over medium heat. Add all the tortillas, stacked, to the skillet. Heat until hot and pliable, rotating them every few seconds with the tongs, for about 1 to 2 minutes.
2. Preheat a heavy skillet, preferably cast-iron, over high heat for 1 to 2 min-utes. Add the oil. When just smoking, after about 30 seconds, add the corn. Cook, stirring frequently, until lightly browned, about 5 minutes. Add the onion and poblano. Reduce the heat to medium and continue cooking just until the onion starts to wilt a little, about 2 to 3 min-utes. Remove from the heat and stir in the tomato and salt and pepper. Set aside.
3. Combine the lobster, mayonnaise, and lime juice in a small bowl. If desired, sea-son with additional salt and pepper.
4. To assemble: Set aside ¼ cup of the corn relish for garnish. Place a handful of lettuce leaves in the center of 2 to 4

plates (4 when serving as a first course, 2 for a meal). Top with the warm tortillas. Place a quarter of the lobster salad and corn relish (or half, if serving as entrees) in the center of each tortilla, then fold in half. Sprinkle each plate with the reserved relish. Serve with lime wedges.
MAKES 2 ENTREES OR 4 FIRST-COURSE WRAPS

Substitutions
Replace lobster with cooked shrimp or crab.

Make Ahead/Take Away
Once assembled, this wrap should be served immediately. However, you can make the corn relish and the lobster salad up to a day ahead and then take them out of the refrigerator 15 to 30 minutes before serving, just to take the chill off. Reseason with salt and pepper if desired. If you like, in addition, heat the relish in the microwave for a minute or until warm.

Jambalaya Wrap

A spicy Louisiana wrap, complete with Creole sauce.

1 8-ounce box Spanish-style rice mix
3 hot turkey sausages (about 8 ounces), sliced
18 medium shrimp (about ½ pound), peeled and deveined
2 teaspoons vegetable oil
1 medium onion, diced
1 green bell pepper, cored, seeded, and diced
3 celery ribs, diced
1 teaspoon Cajun spice
1 14.5-ounce can diced tomatoes, drained
2 teaspoons Worcestershire sauce
½ teaspoon Tabasco or your favorite hot sauce
6 large burrito-size flour tortillas

1. Cook the rice according to the package directions, adding the turkey sausage to the boiling water along with the rice. When the rice is done, after about 25 minutes, stir in the shrimp and replace the lid. (The heat will cook the shrimp.)
2. While the rice is cooking, make the sauce: Heat the oil in a medium skillet over medium heat. Add the onion, half the green pepper, half the celery, and the Cajun spice. Cook, stirring occasionally, until the vegetables are softened, about 5 minutes. Add the tomatoes, Worcestershire sauce, and Tabasco sauce and simmer for an additional 5 minutes.
3. To assemble: Heat the tortillas, one at a time, directly on a gas flame, on a grill, or in a hot skillet, turning frequently, until hot and pliable, about 5 to 15 seconds each. Or heat, stacked, in the microwave (see page 19).

Make 3 wraps at a time: Spread a scant cup of the jambalaya over the center of a tortilla, leaving a 2-inch border. Divide the sauce, remaining diced pepper, and remaining diced celery in half (by eye) and top the rice evenly with a third of the Creole sauce, pepper, and celery. Do not fold in the side, but roll the tortilla into a wrap. Complete the wraps with the remaining ingredients. Or, if you prefer, prepare all at once, assembly-line style. Cut in half on the bias.
MAKES 6 WRAPS

Substitutions
As with so many wraps, almost anything can be thrown into this dish. Try leftover chicken, fish, or meat, diced ham (like tasso), or even cooked beans.

Trim the Fat

This is a low-fat wrap.

Make Ahead/Take Away

Sealed in wax paper, plastic wrap, or foil and refrigerated, the wraps keep for up to a day. Reheat just until warmed through, either sealed in foil in a preheated 350°F oven for 10 to 15 minutes or in the microwave, unsealed, for about 1 minute on high. Serve warm or at room temperature.

Mexican Shrimp Wrap with Two Salsas

 This is a high-return wrap: great flavor for little time and effort.

1 cup white rice
20 medium shrimp (about ½ pound), peeled and deveined
2 tablespoons chopped onion
1 coarsely chopped seeded jalapeño pepper or more to taste
8 ounces tomatillos (8 to 10 large), husked and quartered
1½ teaspoons fresh lime juice
½ teaspoon sugar
¼ teaspoon salt
4 large burrito-size flour tortillas
¼ cup hot salsa or more to taste
¼ cup cilantro leaves

1. Bring 3 quarts salted water to a rapid boil. Add the rice and boil, over high heat, until the rice is just done, after about 18 minutes. Add the shrimp to the rice and continue cooking for about 30 seconds. Strain and let sit in the colander. (The shrimp will continue to cook and flavor the rice.)

2. While the rice is cooking, pulse the onion and jalapeño in a food processor until minced. Add the tomatillos, lime juice, sugar, and salt. Pulse again briefly, just until coarsely chopped. Set aside.

3. To assemble: Heat the tortillas, one at a time, directly on a gas flame, on a grill, or in a hot skillet, turning frequently, until hot and pliable, about 5 to 15 seconds each. Or heat, stacked, in the microwave (see page 19). Spread a tortilla with 1 tablespoon salsa, ½ cup rice, 5 shrimp, and a quarter of the tomatillo sauce and cilantro (plus an additional tablespoon of salsa if you like) in a thick horizontal strip across the bottom third of the tortilla, making sure the ingredients don't quite touch the edges. Fold in the two sides and roll the wrap away from you. Complete the wraps with the remaining ingredients. Or, if you prefer, prepare all at once, assembly-line style. Cut in half on the bias.

MAKES 4 WRAPS

Substitutions

Substitute any kind of fish or seafood for the shrimp.

Trim the Fat
This is a low-fat wrap.

Shortcuts
Skip step 1 and use 2 cups leftover rice and cooked shrimp. Skip step 2 and substitute 1 cup store-bought tomatillo sauce or salsa.

Make Ahead/Take Away
Sealed in wax paper, plastic wrap, or foil and refrigerated, the wraps will keep for up to 4 hours. Reheat just until warmed through, either sealed in foil in a pre-heated 350°F oven for 10 to 15 minutes or in the microwave, unsealed, for about 1 minute on high. Serve warm, cold, or cool (out of the refrigerator for under 30 minutes).

Vietnamese Summer Rolls with Jícama Slaw

 Fresh summer rolls, with their uncooked wrappers, are a light alternative to egg rolls. They use rice paper, which isn't yet widely available, although some supermarkets and most Asian specialty stores stock it. Luckily it keeps indefinitely, so once you're hooked on this and the other rice paper wrap in this book, the Thai Noodle Veggie Wrap (page 82), you'll always keep rice paper in your pantry. Be patient when working with it—after 2 or 3 wraps, you'll get the hang of it, but you're bound to tear a few. Fish sauce is available in the Asian section of the supermarket or in specialty food stores.

FILLING
¾ pound medium shrimp (about 30), peeled, deveined, and cut in half
1 pound jícama, peeled and coarsely grated
2 tablespoons chopped cilantro leaves
2 tablespoons chopped fresh mint leaves
2 teaspoons fish sauce
2 teaspoons fresh lime juice
¼ teaspoon hot red pepper flakes
⅛ teaspoon salt or to taste

DIPPING SAUCE
2 tablespoons fresh lime juice
1 tablespoon rice wine vinegar
1 tablespoon fish sauce
1 tablespoon sugar
¼ teaspoon hot red pepper flakes

about 20 7-inch round rice paper wrapped

1. Bring a small pot of lightly salted water to a rapid boil. Add the shrimp and drain after 30 seconds. (They will continue to cook in their own heat.)

2. Toss the shrimp and jícama in a large bowl with the cilantro, mint, 2 teaspoons fish sauce, 2 teaspoons lime juice, ¼ teaspoon red pepper flakes, and salt. Let sit for 10 minutes to blend the flavors, then transfer the ingredients to a colander and press out extra liquid with a wooden spoon.

3. While the filling is sitting, make the Dipping Sauce: Combine the 2 tablespoons lime juice, vinegar, 1 tablespoon fish sauce, sugar, and ¼ teaspoon red pepper flakes in a small bowl. Set aside.

4. Place a large, absorbent dish towel on a work surface. Fill a medium bowl with warm water and submerge 2 to 3 sheets of rice paper in the water, one at a time. When soft and pliable but not mushy, after about 1 minute, pull them out and pat dry. Arrange the sheets on the towel. Place about 1 rounded tablespoon of drained filling at one end. Fold over the filling, pulling the filling toward the edge of the rice paper to compact it a little,

then fold in the sides and roll away from you. Complete 3 or 4 wraps at a time with the remaining ingredients. Serve immediately or chill and serve cold with Dipping Sauce.

MAKES ABOUT 20 SMALL WRAPS

Trim the Fat
This is a low-fat wrap.

Shortcuts
Skip step 1 and use precooked shrimp cut in half.

Make Ahead/Take Away
Serve immediately or chill, well covered, to prevent toughening of the skins, up to 4 to 6 hours ahead. Once chilled, these hold together very well for travel.

Savory Shrimp and Feta with Fennel Confit

 The timeless pairing of fennel and seafood, sprinkled with feta cheese, makes a refined wrap.

2 small fennel bulbs
2 tablespoons olive oil
4 large garlic cloves, sliced
¼ teaspoon fennel seeds
pinch of salt
20 medium shrimp (about ½ pound), peeled and deveined
¼ cup crumbled feta cheese
2 tablespoons fresh lemon juice
4 large burrito-size flour tortillas

1. Remove the tough outer leaves from the fennel bulbs, then quarter, core, and dice the bulbs. Chop the green fennel fronds and reserve ¼ cup of the chopped greens. Heat the oil in a small saucepan over medium heat. Add three quarters of the chopped fennel, reserving the remaining fennel and chopped fronds in a small bowl. Stir the garlic, fennel seeds, and salt into the saucepan. Cook over medium-low heat, stirring occasionally, until the fennel is lightly browned, 10 to 15 minutes. Add ¼ cup water, reduce the heat to low, cover, and simmer until the fennel is very tender, about 10 minutes longer. Add the shrimp, stirring frequently, just until cooked through, about 5 minutes.

2. While the fennel is cooking, add the feta and lemon juice to the reserved raw fennel and fronds. Stir to combine.

3. To assemble: Heat the tortillas, one at a time, directly on a gas flame, on a grill, or in a hot skillet, turning frequently, until hot and pliable about 5 to 15 seconds each. Or heat, stacked, in the microwave (see page 19). Distribute a quarter of the shrimp and fennel, topped with a quarter of the feta mixture, in a thick horizontal strip across the bottom third of a tortilla, making sure the ingredients don't quite touch the edges. Fold in the two sides and roll the wrap away from you. Complete the wraps with the remaining ingredients. Or, if you prefer, prepare all at once, assembly-line style. Cut in half on the bias.
MAKES 4 WRAPS

Trim the Fat

This is a low-fat wrap if the oil and feta are cut in half. To replace the lost moisture, add 2 extra tablespoons of water or chicken stock to step 2. Salt to taste if necessary.

Make Ahead/Take Away

These wraps are best eaten within 15 minutes of assembling. Do not reheat. If you wish to eat them cold, store the wraps, well sealed in wax paper, plastic wrap, or foil, in the refrigerator for up to 2 hours.

Zydeco Shrimp

 A wrap with plenty of punch! Southern flavors are always popular, and shrimp takes well to this classic combination of ingredients.

1 cup white rice
2 teaspoons vegetable oil
1 small onion, diced
1 green bell pepper, cored, seeded, and diced
2 celery ribs, diced
1 8-ounce can tomato sauce
2 teaspoons Worcestershire sauce
2 teaspoons hot sauce or more to taste
20 medium shrimp (about ½ pound), peeled and deveined
4 large burrito-size flour tortillas
4 scallions, both white and green parts, trimmed, cut in half lengthwise, and sliced into 1-inch pieces

1. Bring 3 quarts salted water to a rolling boil. Add the rice and boil it until the rice is cooked, about 18 minutes. Drain.

2. Heat the oil in a medium skillet over medium heat. Add the onion, half the green pepper, and half the celery. Cook, stirring occasionally, until the onion is translucent, about 5 minutes. Add the tomato sauce, Worcestershire sauce, and hot sauce. Continue to cook to blend the flavors, about 5 minutes. Stir in the shrimp and cook until just done, stirring frequently, about 2 minutes. (Be careful not to overcook.)

3. To assemble: Heat the tortillas, one at a time, directly on a gas flame, on a grill, or in a hot skillet, turning frequently, until hot and pliable, about 5 to 15 seconds each. Or heat, stacked, in the microwave (see page 19). Lay a tortilla on a 12-inch square of foil. Layer ½ cup of the rice, a quarter of the shrimp mixture, a quarter of the raw pepper and celery, and a quarter of the scallions in a thick horizontal strip across the bottom third of the tortilla, making sure the ingredients don't quite touch the edges. Fold in the two sides and roll the wrap away from you, being careful not to include the foil in the spiral. Complete the wraps with the remaining ingredients. Or, if you prefer, prepare all at once, assembly-line style. Cut in half on the bias.

MAKES 4 WRAPS

Trim the Fat
This is a low-fat wrap.

Make Ahead/Take Away
Prepare the sauce, up to the point where the shrimp is added, up to 2 days in advance and chill. Once assembled, this wrap can be refrigerated for 6 hours.

Reheat just until warmed through, either sealed in foil in a preheated 350°F oven for 10 to 15 minutes or in the microwave, unsealed, for about 1 minute on high. Serve warm.

Pepper-Seared Scallops with Oranges

 The sweetness of fresh oranges are a natural foil for the spicy sea scallops.

1 teaspoon peppercorns
½ pound sea scallops
1 navel orange, skin and white pith removed with a knife, flesh cut into rounds
2 teaspoons olive oil
2 very thin slices of red onion
¼ cup cilantro leaves
2 tablespoons fresh lime juice
salt to taste
2 large burrito-size flour tortillas
1 endive bulb, trimmed and slivered lengthwise

1. Crush the peppercorns with the bottom of a heavy pot. Remove the muscle (the small, tough tendon) from the scallops. Add the scallops to a small bowl with the crushed pepper and the oranges, breaking the oranges up with your hands. Be careful not to mush the scallops.

2. Heat the oil in a nonstick skillet over high heat until very hot. Add the scallops and sear on both sides until browned, about 1 minute total. Remove from the heat and immediately add the oranges, their juice, the onion, cilantro, and lime juice, shaking the pan to combine. Season with salt.

3. To assemble: Heat the tortillas, one at a time, directly on a gas flame, on a grill, or in a hot skillet, turning frequently, until hot and pliable, about 5 to 15 seconds each. Or heat, stacked, in the microwave (see page 19). Distribute half the scallop mixture and endive in a thick horizontal strip about a third of the way up from the bottom of the tortillas, making sure the ingredients don't quite touch the edges. Roll the thin wrap away from you. Cut in half on the bias.
MAKES 2 WRAPS

Make Ahead/Take Away
Serve immediately.

Scallop Vegetable Stir-Fry with Black Bean Sauce

 For a quick but satisfying meal, try this wok wrap. Black bean sauce can be found in the Asian section of most supermarkets or in specialty food stores.

½ pound sea scallops
2 teaspoons vegetable oil
2 to 3 ounces (1 handful) green beans, ends snapped off
¼ cup ½-inch red bell pepper strips
2 teaspoons minced peeled fresh ginger
1 small garlic clove, chopped
1 teaspoon black bean sauce
2 large burrito-size flour tortillas
2 scallions, both white and green parts, trimmed and sliced diagonally

1. Remove the muscle (the small, tough tendon) from the scallops and cut the scallops in half horizontally. Preheat a wok or large skillet over high heat for about 30 seconds. Add the oil, green beans, and red peppers. Stir-fry for about 1 minute, then add the scallops, ginger, and garlic. Continue stirring until the scallops just begin to turn opaque, about 1 to 2 minutes longer. Stir in the bean sauce.

2. To assemble: Heat the tortillas, one at a time, directly on a gas flame, on a grill, or in a hot skillet, turning frequently, until hot and pliable, about 5 to 15 seconds each. Or heat, stacked, in the microwave (see page 19). Distribute half of the scallop mixture in a thick horizontal strip across the bottom third of each tortilla, making sure the ingredients don't quite touch the edges. Fold in the two sides and roll the wraps away from you. Cut in half on the bias.

MAKES 2 WRAPS

Trim the Fat
This wrap has very little fat, but for an even lower fat wrap, use a nonstick wok and cut the oil in half.

Make Ahead/Take Away
Best eaten immediately.

Panfried Catfish Tacos with Cool Cabbage Slaw

 A down-home casual meal for a hot summer day or any time at all. I love how the corny flavor from the crisp cornmeal breading on the catfish echoes the steamed corn tortilla. A good-quality hot sauce makes all the difference.

4 corn tortillas
1½ cups sliced cabbage (about ¼ small head)
⅓ cup coarsely chopped flat-leaf parsley
3 tablespoons mayonnaise
7 teaspoons grainy mustard
2 teaspoons cider vinegar
salt to taste
8 ounces boneless, skinless catfish, cut into 2- by 1-inch fingers
1 rounded tablespoon cornmeal, preferably stone-ground
2 teaspoons vegetable oil
hot sauce to taste

1. Wrap the tortillas well in a kitchen towel. Set in a steamer above boiling water. Cover well and steam for 1 minute, then turn off the heat and let sit until warm and pliable, about 15 minutes. (These will stay warm for a while.) Alternatively, wet your hands and rub them across each tortilla. Heat a skillet over medium heat. Add all the tortillas, stacking them together in the skillet. Heat until they become hot and pliable, rotating them every few seconds with tongs, about 1 to 2 minutes.

2. Combine the cabbage, parsley, mayonnaise, 2 tablespoons of the mustard, and the vinegar in a bowl. Toss well and add salt. Set aside.

3. Toss the catfish in the remaining teaspoon of mustard. Sprinkle with cornmeal and a pinch of salt and toss again to coat. Heat the oil in a large nonstick skillet over medium-high heat. Add the catfish and cook, turning once, until crisp on both sides and just cooked all the way through, about 1 minute on each side.

4. To assemble: Take catfish fingers, slaw, hot sauce, and warm tortillas to the table for diners to assemble themselves. (Alternatively, lay down a tortilla. Top with a quarter of the slaw and catfish in a strip down the center. Season with lots of hot sauce and roll from left to right.

MAKES 4 TACOS, SERVING 2

Substitutions

Replace catfish with any mild, flaky, white fish.

Shortcuts

Replace the homemade slaw with 1 cup store-bought coleslaw.

Make Ahead/Take Away

The slaw may be made ahead and refrigerated. Once assembled, serve the wraps immediately. These are fabulous, but sloppy to eat.

Provençal Wrap

 Gutsy salt cod and garlic mayonnaise, called *aïoli,* are culinary staples of southern France. For this rustic wrap, roasted red pepper is added to the sauce, turning it into a rouille, or red pepper mayonnaise, which is the traditional accompaniment to bouillabaisse. The addition of steamed asparagus and ripe tomatoes creates a unique summer wrap. Look for salt cod in the fish section of a well-stocked supermarket or at your fishmonger. The unsoaked leftover cod will keep, refrigerated for 2 days. If you buy more asparagus than you need for this recipe, steam the rest the next day and serve the remaining rouille as a dip.

½ pound salt cod
1 egg
1½ teaspoons Dijon mustard
⅓ cup olive oil, plus extra for brushing pita
4 garlic cloves, peeled
1 tablespoon fresh lemon juice
½ 7½-ounce jar roasted red peppers, drained, rinsed, and patted dry
1 slice of white bread
salt and cayenne pepper to taste
½ pound asparagus, tough ends removed
2 ripe tomatoes, cut into wedges
4 pocketless pitas

1. Soak the cod in a large bowl of ice water the day before preparing it, changing the water once or twice.

2. Make the rouille in a food processor or blender. Blend the egg and mustard until frothy. With the motor running, add ⅓ cup of the oil in a thin stream, then add the garlic, lemon juice, roasted red peppers, and bread. Season with salt and cayenne and blend until smooth. Set aside.

3. Preheat the broiler. Bring a large pot of water to a boil. Drain the cod, add to the boiling water for 1 minute, then drain again (this will remove excess salt). Bring a fresh pot of water to a boil. Add the asparagus. Cook for 3 minutes or until the asparagus are a little underdone. Add the salt cod and reduce to a low simmer, until the asparagus are tender-crisp, about 2 to 4 minutes longer. Drain the asparagus and cod.

4. To assemble: Brush one side of each pita lightly with oil. Broil, oiled side up,

until slightly crisp but not brittle, about 1 minute. Set each pita, crisp side down, on top of a 12-inch square of foil. Shake the colander to drain any remaining liquid from the cod and asparagus, then divide them, along with the tomatoes, equally among the pita breads in a strip down the center of each. Pour about 2½ tablespoons of the rouille on top of each pita, then wrap into a cone, using the foil as support and to seal the bottom.
MAKES 4 WRAPS

Substitutions
If salt cod is unavailable, or if you prefer a milder taste, substitute fresh for salt cod.

Skip the soaking and 1-minute blanching and draining process and just add the fresh cod in step 3 for the final cooking.

Make Ahead/Take Away
Soaking the cod and making the rouille—steps 1 and 2—may be done a day or 2 in advance, then the ingredients should be stored in the refrigerator. When you are ready to eat, let the rouille sit out at room temperature for 15 minutes, then proceed as described.

Roasted Salmon-Asparagus Roll

 Caramelized onion and honey mustard pump up the flavor in this succulent roll. I've served it for an elegant Fourth of July concert-picnic, with a simple rice salad and chilled white wine.

12 large or medium asparagus (about ¾ pound), tough ends removed
8 ¾- to 1-inch-thick slices of onion, broken up into rings (about 2 small onions)
1 tablespoon olive oil
1 teaspoon freshly ground pepper
½ teaspoon salt
¾ pound skinless salmon fillet
2 tablespoons fresh lemon juice
1½ tablespoons honey
1½ tablespoons grainy mustard
4 small taco-size flour tortillas

1. Preheat the oven 425°F. In a small baking dish, toss the asparagus, onion, and oil with the pepper and salt. Roast, uncovered, until the onion starts to brown, about 10 minutes. Add the salmon, turning once to coat, and roast until it is still slightly raw in the center or just cooked through, as you prefer, 6 to 8 minutes. Remove from oven and set aside until cool enough to handle. (If the salmon is too hot, it will make the wrap soggy.) Turn oven down to 350°F.

2. While the salmon is cooking, combine the lemon juice, honey, and mustard in a medium bowl. Add the cooked salmon, asparagus, and onion and toss gently to combine.

3. To assemble: Stack the tortillas, wrap them in foil, and heat in a 350°F oven, just until warm and pliable, about 3 to 5 minutes. (Do not overheat, or they will become brittle.) Or heat the tortillas, one at a time, directly on a gas flame, on a grill, or in a hot skillet, turning frequently, until hot and pliable, about 5 to 15 seconds each. Distribute a quarter of the salmon mixture in a thick horizontal strip across the bottom third of the tortillas, making sure the ingredients don't quite touch the edges. Roll away from you into a wrap (do not fold in the sides). Cut in half on the bias.

MAKES 4 WRAPS

Substitutions

If you have honey mustard around, replace the honey and mustard with 3 tablespoons honey mustard. Mountain bread also works well in this recipe.

Make Ahead/Take Away

This wrap is good served warm or cold, so you can eat immediately or seal it in wax paper, plastic wrap, or foil and refrigerate, for up to 6 hours (this does not reheat well). For the best flavor, remove from the refrigerator 15 minutes before serving.

Teriyaki-Glazed Salmon Spirals

 This Japanese-inspired wrap is a household favorite. The pink color and rich flavor of the salmon are offset by the bite of greens and horseradish. The folding technique prevents dripping and allows the pretty kale leaves to peek out the top. Don't worry about using up the beer; the recipe calls for ⅓ cup, but the rest goes well with the finished wrap.

⅓ cup beer
¼ cup plus 1 tablespoon rice wine vinegar
1 tablespoon plus 1 teaspoon sugar
1 tablespoon soy sauce
1 7- to 8-ounce skinless salmon fillet
2 teaspoons drained bottled horseradish
4 small taco-size flour tortillas
8 kale leaves, 3 to 4 inches of the frilly tops only
4 medium radishes, cut in half and thinly sliced

1. Preheat a grill to medium-high heat or preheat the broiler, setting the rack close to the heat.

2. Whisk together the beer, ¼ cup of the vinegar, the sugar, and the soy sauce in a skillet. Marinate the salmon fillet in the skillet for 10 minutes, turning once.

3. Remove the salmon from the marinade and broil or grill it until it is still a little raw in the middle or just cooked through, as you prefer, about 2 to 3 minutes on each side.

4. While the salmon is cooling, boil the marinade in the skillet, stirring frequently and watching closely to prevent burning, until it is reduced to about a third of the original amount, after about 2 minutes. Stir in the remaining tablespoon of vine-gar and the horseradish. Remove from the heat and allow to cool.

5. To assemble: Heat the tortillas, one at a time, directly on a gas flame, on a grill, or in a hot skillet, turning frequently, until hot and pliable, about 5 to 15 sec-onds each. Or heat, stacked, in the microwave (see page 19). Spread a tortilla with about 1 tablespoon of the sauce. Place 2 kale leaves on a tortilla, one stick-ing out over the right edge. Distribute a quarter of the grilled salmon (flaked by hand) and the radish slices over the sauce, drizzled over the top, in a thick horizontal strip across the bottom third of the tortilla. Fold in the left side of the tor-tilla a quarter of the way, and roll the wrap from the bottom. Complete the wraps with the remaining ingredients. Or, if you prefer, prepare all at once, assembly-line style.

MAKES 4 WRAPS

Make Ahead/Take Away

Sealed in wax paper, plastic wrap, or foil and refrigerated, the wraps keep for up to a day. Serve warm, cold, or cool (out of the refrigerator for under 30 minutes).

Wasabi-Steamed Salmon and Cabbage Bundles

 Effortless but impressive, this attractive knife-and-fork wrap, cut on the bias, makes a healthful and elegant light lunch or first course. Cook up to a day in advance and chill, then leave out at room temperature for 15 minutes before serving. Both wasabi (Japanese horseradish) and pickled ginger, once hard to track down, are now widely available in the Asian section of supermarkets and at specialty stores. Occasionally pickled ginger is available unsweetened—for this recipe, be sure you buy the type with sugar listed in the ingredients.

4 large green cabbage leaves, removed from the outside of the head
1 pound skinless salmon fillet bones removed
salt to taste
4 teaspoons wasabi powder
¼ cup pickled ginger strips
2 tablespoons juice from pickled ginger
3 tablespoons rice wine vinegar
1 scallion, both white and green parts, trimmed and minced
¾ teaspoon Asian sesame oil

1. Place the cabbage leaves in a steamer over boiling water. Cover and steam until softened enough to roll, about 5 minutes. Turn the heat down to a simmer.
2. While the cabbage is steaming, trim every bit of gray fat from the salmon. Cut the fish into 4 long strips.
3. To assemble: Lay the cabbage leaves down on a clean counter. Place a strip of salmon along the spine of each leaf. Sprinkle each with a pinch of salt and a teaspoon of wasabi. Lay a tablespoon of the pickled ginger over and around each salmon strip. Fold in the sides of the cabbage and roll up as tightly as possible. Bring the steamer water back to a boil and place the rolls in the steamer, seam side down. Cover, then turn off the heat and let sit for 8 minutes for medium, 10 to 12 minutes for well done. (The salmon shouldn't be cooked through, but just translucent in the center.) Chill, well wrapped, for at least 45 minutes or up to 24 hours.
4. Mix the ginger juice, vinegar, scallion, and sesame oil in a small bowl.
5. To serve, cut each bundle in half on the bias with a sharp knife. For a pretty

presentation, prop one half-bundle over the other. Pour a quarter of the sauce over each bundle.

MAKES 4 WRAPS

Substitutions

If you can find only tightly packed pickled ginger or you don't have 2 tablespoons of juice in your jar, add 1 tablespoon pickled ginger juice and 1 additional tablespoon rice wine vinegar.

Make Ahead/Take Away

Serve immediately or serve cold; these don't reheat well. Sealed in plastic wrap, wax paper, or foil and refrigerated, the wraps will keep for up to a day.

New York Brunch Wrap

 At least once a month my relatives schlepped up to the suburbs from the Bronx bearing smoked fish they had purchased from "the old neighborhood" on the Lower East Side of Manhattan. This Eastern European feast always featured numerous treats, including lox and cream cheese on bagels, along with thick slices of sweet onion and ripe tomatoes. Playing on this nostalgic Sunday brunch theme, I created a contemporary wrap that makes a satisfying lunch or do-ahead appetizer.

4 small taco-size flour tortillas
½ cup cream cheese, softened
4 ounces thinly sliced smoked salmon (about 8 slices)
2 plum tomatoes, coarsely chopped
4 paper-thin slices from a small red onion
2 tablespoons coarsely chopped fresh dill
1 tablespoons drained capers
1 lemon
freshly ground pepper to taste

To assemble: Heat the tortillas, one at a time, directly on a gas flame, on a grill, or in a hot skillet, turning frequently, until hot and pliable, 5 to 15 seconds each. Or heat, stacked, in the microwave (see page 19). Spread a tortilla with a quarter of the cream cheese, leaving about a ½-inch border. Top the cheese with an even layer of a quarter of the smoked salmon, tomatoes, onion, dill, and capers, a generous squeeze of lemon, and several grinds of pepper. Roll tightly, pressing firmly to seal. Slice off the ends, then cut in half or into thirds on the bias for a meal or into 6 to 8 spirals per roll for appetizers (if serving as appetizers, chill for about 15 minutes before slicing). Complete wraps with the remaining ingredients. Or, if you prefer, prepare all at once, assembly-line style.

MAKES 4 ROLLS, SERVING 4 AS LUNCH OR 10 TO 12 AS AN APPETIZER

Make Ahead/Take Away

Sealed in wax paper, foil, or plastic wrap and refrigerated, the wraps keep well for up to a day. If you are using them for an appetizer, slice slightly chilled: Refrigerate, slice, and then, for the best flavor, leave out of the refrigerator for 30 minutes to 1 hour.

Seared Tuna Amandine

 This subtle, elegant wrap demands rare, very fresh tuna.

1 tablespoon olive oil
1 large handful of green beans, stem ends snapped off
2 tablespoons sliced almonds
1 garlic clove, chopped
6 ounces tuna, 1 inch thick, cut into 1-inch strips
2 tablespoons fresh lemon juice
salt and freshly ground pepper to taste
2 large burrito-size flour tortillas

1. Heat 2 teaspoons of the olive oil in a large skillet over medium heat. Add the beans, almonds, and garlic. Cook, stirring frequently, until the almonds and garlic begin to toast, about 1 minute. (Don't cook too long, or the garlic will burn.) Turn off the heat.

2. Heat the remaining teaspoon olive oil in a separate heavy skillet over medium-high heat. Add the tuna and sear briefly, about 15 seconds on each side, or to the desired doneness. Transfer to the skillet with the beans. Stir in the lemon juice and salt and pepper.

3. Heat the tortillas, one at a time, directly on a gas flame, on a grill, or in the skillet used to cook the beans, turning frequently, until hot and pliable, about 5 to 15 seconds each. Or heat, stacked, in the microwave (see page 19). Distribute half the filling in a thick horizontal strip across the bottom third of each tortilla, making sure the ingredients don't quite touch the edges (do not fold in the sides). Roll away from you into a tight, thin wrap. Cut in half on the bias.
MAKES 2 WRAPS

Make Ahead/Take Away
Sealed in wax paper, plastic wrap, or foil and refrigerated, these wraps will keep for up to 6 hours. Good hot, at room temperature, or cold. Serve chilled wraps with a wedge of lemon.

9 meat wraps

The hearty meat wraps in this chapter cover a wide range of robust flavors, from Tangier Lamb Tagine with Spiced Yogurt to Rib-Stickin', Finger-Lickin' Pulled Pork with its southern barbecue twang. They go well beyond the common sandwich, rolling linguiça sausage and kale into the Portuguese Roll and cumin-seared lamb and cool yogurt-cucumber sauce into the Athenian Lamb Gyro with Tzatziki.

The emphasis here is on flavor. After all, many of us, in keeping with today's guidelines for less meat consumption, have cut down on meat. So when we settle down to the occasional meat meal, we demand real satisfaction and deep flavor, and these recipes fit the bill.

Nevertheless, if you want to scale down the fat in these wraps, there are plenty of suggestions for substituting leaner cuts, such as ground turkey in the Diner Wrap or low-fat sausage in the Alsatian Roll. For balance, many of these meat rolls are also packed with veggies of some kind, like crunchy greens, so they provide a total meal-in-a-wrap. And there are recipes where the vegetables star (or costar) and the meat provides supporting flavor, like the bacon in the Southern Roll.

It's easy to improvise your own meat wrap variations with leftovers or deli-sliced meat. Meat holds up to big, bright flavors, so liberally add condiments and sauces you have on hand, like pickled jalapeños, hoisin sauce, and Dijon mustard (see lists on pages 14 to 15). To provide textural variety and balance, you can add a multitude of accompaniments, from freshly steamed broccoli to yesterday's salad. Ingredients like these might cause a regular bread sandwich to disintegrate. Luckily, the nature of wraps means they'll hold together quite well as long as you keep the filling pieces reasonably small.

While a few of these wraps are long simmered, most are quick to assemble, especially the Panini Wrap, Carnegie Deli Wrap, Parisian Pocket, and Joy Luck Pocket. Wraps are a great way to make the most of meat without overindulging—so enjoy!

MEAT

Alsatian Roll

Potato and Chorizo Taco

Portuguese Roll

Southern Roll

Rib-Stickin', Finger-Lickin' Pulled Pork

Bourbon-Glazed Pork with Caramelized Onions

Parisian Pocket

Diner Wrap

Carnegie Deli Wrap

Joy Luck Pocket

Spice-Blackened Steak Gyro with Pickled Onions

Tangier Lamb Tagine with Spiced Yogurt

Athenian Lamb Gyro with Tzatziki

Just-Like-Mom's Lamb Gyro

Panini Wrap

Alsatian Roll

 Try this sophisticated variation of franks and sauerkraut with an icy glass of wheat beer. This hearty recipe makes 8 wraps that hold well, but the recipe is also easily cut in half for a smaller crowd.

8 medium new potatoes (about 2 pounds)
2 tablespoons unsalted butter
2 large Spanish onions, coarsely chopped (about 4 cups)
1 pound knockwurst (about 4 links), quartered lengthwise and sliced
½ cup cider vinegar
1 small head of green cabbage, tough outer leaves removed, quartered, cored, and cut into ½-inch slices
1 tablespoon brown sugar
1 teaspoon salt
8 large burrito-size flour tortillas
3 tablespoons grainy mustard
2 Granny Smith or other tart apples, cored and thinly sliced

1. Cover the potatoes with salted water in a medium pot. Bring to a boil and cook until fork-tender, 20 to 25 minutes. Drain.

2. While the potatoes are cooking, melt the butter in a large saucepan over medium heat. Add the onions and knockwurst and cook, stirring occasionally, until lightly browned, about 10 to 15 minutes. Add the vinegar, stirring to scrape up the browned bits. Add the cabbage, brown sugar, and salt. Cook, covered, until the cabbage is slightly tender but still crunchy, about 10 minutes.

3. To assemble: Heat the tortillas, one at a time, directly on a gas flame, on a grill, or in a hot skillet, turning frequently, until hot and pliable, about 5 to 15 seconds each. Or heat, stacked, in the microwave (see page 19). Spread a tortilla with a rounded teaspoon of mustard. Layer with a potato (mashed right onto the tortilla with a fork), an eighth of the knockwurst-cabbage mixture, and an eighth of the apple in a thick horizontal strip across the bottom third of the tortillas, making sure the ingredients don't quite touch the edges. Fold in the two sides and roll the wrap away from you. Complete the wraps with the remaining ingredients. Or, if you prefer, prepare all at once (or 4 at a time), assembly-line style. Cut in half on the bias.

MAKES 8 WRAPS

Make Ahead/Take Away

The filling can be made a day in advance and then assembled before it is eaten. Sealed in wax paper, plastic wrap, or foil and refrigerated, the wraps will keep well for up to 8 hours. Reheat just until warmed through, either sealed in foil in a preheated 350°F oven for 10 to 15 minutes or in the microwave, unsealed, for about 1 minute on high.

Potato and Chorizo Taco

 This is a quick version of a classic Mexican combination. The neutral flavor of the potatoes is a perfect contrast to the spicy chorizo sausages. (Chorizo can be found in supermarket meat cases.) The tortilla filling may be made ahead and reheated, but once it's assembled, eat it right away.

1 chorizo sausage (6 to 8 ounces), thinly sliced
1 baking potato (about ½ pound), cut into ½-inch dice
½ medium onion, sliced
1 plum tomato, coarsely chopped
salt and freshly ground pepper to taste
4 small taco-size flour tortillas
4 to 8 lettuce leaves, any kind, optional

1. In a large skillet, over medium-high heat cook the chorizo, stirring occasionally to break it up, until it starts to render its fat, about 5 minutes.

2. Stir in the potato, onion, and ⅔ cup water. Reduce the heat to medium and cook, covered well, stirring occasionally, and adding a little water if necessary to prevent sticking. When the potatoes are soft, after 10 to 15 minutes, remove from the heat.

3. Using a potato masher or fork, mash the sausage-potato mixture slightly right in the pan. Stir in the tomato. Season with salt and pepper.

4. To assemble: Heat the tortillas, one at a time, directly on a gas flame, on a grill, or in a hot skillet, turning frequently, until hot and pliable, about 5 to 15 seconds each. Or heat, stacked, in the microwave (see page 19). Lay a quarter of the filling in a strip down the center of a warm tortilla and roll from left to right. Complete the wraps with the remaining ingredients. Or, if you prefer, prepare all at once, assembly-line style.

MAKES 4 WRAPS

Substitutions
Use corn tortillas instead of flour.

Trim the Fat
To reduce the fat, use lower-fat sausages.

Make Ahead/Take Away
The filling can be made up to 3 days ahead and reheated, covered, in the microwave, just until warm, about 2 to 5 minutes on high, or on the stove. Once the wraps are assembled, serve them warm and eat immediately.

Portuguese Roll

 On my annual visit to Cape Cod, where there's a large Portuguese population, I'm sure to savor a bowl of their famous national soup, *caldo verde*, brimming with luscious linguiça sausages and kale. This meal-in-one wrap is a tribute to the fine combination of those rich spicy sausages and strong sharp greens. The wrap calls for uncooked pizza dough, which is widely available both fresh and frozen in supermarkets.

4 large kale leaves, tough spines removed, rolled and cut into 1-inch strips (about 2 cups packed)
1 medium onion, chopped
8 to 10 imported black olives, pitted and roughly chopped
1½ teaspoons red wine vinegar
½ teaspoon freshly ground pepper
½ pound linguiça sausages, cut into quarters lengthwise and diced
olive oil for the baking sheet
2 tablespoons cornmeal
flour for dusting
1 pound pizza dough at room temperature

1. Preheat the oven to 400°F. Combine the kale, onion, olives, vinegar, and pepper in a large bowl. Toss well. Add the linguiça and toss again. Set aside.

2. Generously oil a baking sheet and sprinkle it with cornmeal. Lightly flour a clean surface. With your hands, shape the pizza dough into a square and roll with a rolling pin to form a roughly 10- by 13-inch rectangle. Transfer to the baking sheet.

3. To assemble and cook: Spread the filling evenly over the dough, leaving a 2-inch border. Roll into a spiral and, with the seam down, tuck the ends under to

seal. Transfer to the prepared baking sheet and allow to rest for 20 to 30 minutes. Bake until well browned, 20 to 25 minutes. Slice with a serrated knife and serve immediately.

MAKES 1 LARGE ROLL, SERVING 4 TO 6

Make Ahead/Take Away
The filling can be made a day in advance and stored in the refrigerator. Once assembled, keep the roll at room temperature for up to 2 hours before baking. Once baked, this should be served immediately.

Southern Roll

 This is a BLT with a Dixie twist. It is a meal in one, but you can also make it part of a feast in the late summer, served with corn on the cob and black-eyed peas, or in the winter, with any kind of bean soup.

1 pound sweet potatoes (about 1 large or 2 small)
8 strips of bacon
⅓ cup chopped pecans
1 garlic clove, peeled and smashed
1 bunch of kale leaves, tough ends and spines removed, coarsely chopped
3 tablespoons red wine vinegar
1 teaspoon hot red pepper flakes
¼ teaspoon salt
4 rounds of mountain bread
Tabasco or your favorite hot sauce, to taste

1. Pierce the sweet potatoes with a fork and microwave on high until very soft, 10 to 15 minutes. When cool enough to handle, halve lengthwise and peel off the skin.

2. While the sweet potatoes are cooking, place the bacon in a wok or large skillet over medium-high heat and cook, stirring frequently, until crisp, about 5 minutes. Remove with tongs, crumble, and reserve bacon in a small bowl. Pour off and discard the fat. Add the nuts to the pan and cook over medium-high heat, stirring continuously, until they are toasted, about 2 to 3 minutes. Transfer to the bowl with the bacon.

3. Stir in the garlic and kale, with some of the water clinging to it, vinegar, red pepper flakes, and salt. Increase the heat to high, add 2 tablespoons water, and stir continuously until the kale is bright green and just starting to wilt, about 3 minutes. Remove from the heat and discard the garlic.

4. To assemble: Warm the mountain bread in a hot skillet, turning frequently, just until hot and pliable, about 15 to 20 seconds each. Layer a quarter of the sweet potato (smashed with a fork right into the bread), kale, bacon, and nuts in a thick horizontal strip across the bottom third of the tortillas, making sure the ingredients don't quite touch the edges. Roll away from you. Complete the wraps with the remaining ingredients. Or, if you prefer, prepare all at once, assembly-line

style. Cut in half on the bias. Serve with plenty of Tabasco or hot sauce.
MAKES 4 WRAPS

Trim the Fat
This is a low-fat wrap if half the bacon is replaced with low-fat turkey bacon. Be sure to pour off any remaining fat from the wok or skillet.

Make Ahead/Take Away
All the ingredients can be prepared up to a day in advance. Reheat everything but the nuts just until warmed through, separately but on the same plate covered with an inverted bowl, in the microwave on high. Assemble. If assembled ahead, chill for up to 3 hours. Reheat just until warmed through, either sealed in foil in a preheated 350°F oven for 10 to 15 minutes or in the microwave, unsealed, for about 1 minute on high.

Rib-Stickin', Finger-Lickin' Pulled Pork

 Imagine this—savory pork ribs in a sticky beer and barbecue sauce, wrapped up with crunchy coleslaw and tangy kale. These do take longer than the other recipes in this book, but perfect ribs are worth the wait. Besides, they can be left almost unattended while they simmer or made up to 5 days in advance.

1 tablespoon vegetable oil
2¼ to 2½ pounds country-style boneless pork ribs
1 12-ounce bottle beer, preferably dark
1 cup barbecue sauce any kind
1 medium onion, diced
1 tablespoon red wine vinegar or more to taste
4 large burrito-size flour tortillas
3 kale leaves, spines removed, rolled and thinly sliced, optional
¾ cup coleslaw (about 8 ounces)

1. Heat the oil in a large skillet over high heat. Add the ribs and brown thoroughly on both sides, turning as necessary, for about 10 to 12 minutes in all. Pour off any fat that has accumulated.

2. Add the beer, barbecue sauce, and onion. Simmer over medium-low heat, well covered, until the pork is very tender, about 1 hour. Uncover and boil for 10 to 20 minutes or until the sauce is thick. Remove the meat from the skillet and pour off all the fat from the sauce (there will be a lot). When the meat is cool enough to handle, shred it, discarding any remaining fat. Return the meat to the sauce and stir in the vinegar, scraping up any browned bits from the bottom of the skillet.

3. To assemble: Heat the tortillas, one at a time, directly on a gas flame, on a grill, or in a hot skillet, turning frequently, until hot and pliable, about 5 to 15 seconds each. Or heat, stacked, in the microwave (see page 19). Lay a tortilla down on a 12-inch square of foil. Layer a quarter of the kale, meat, and coleslaw in a thick horizontal strip across the bottom third of the tortillas, making sure the ingredients don't quite touch the edges. Fold in the two sides and roll the wrap away from you, being careful not to include the foil in the spiral. When the spiral is complete, wrap with foil for support. Complete the wraps with the remaining ingredients. Or, if you prefer, prepare all at once, assembly-line style. Peel down the foil as you eat.

MAKES 4 LARGE WRAPS

Make Ahead/Take Away

Make the pork filling up to 5 days in advance and chill. Reheat in the microwave on high, covered, until warm, about 2 to 5 minutes. Assemble as described and serve immediately.

Bourbon-Glazed Pork
with Caramelized Onions

 Even after a day of testing recipes, I stood by the stove devouring this dark-tasting pork and onion wrap, offset by the bright flavor of a nectarine and watercress salad. If you don't stock bourbon, all liquor stores sell tiny "nip" bottles.

1½ tablespoons olive oil
1 very small pork tenderloin (10 ounces)
2 large onions, sliced (about 2 cups)
½ teaspoon salt or more to taste
½ teaspoon freshly ground pepper or more to taste
2 tablespoons bourbon
½ cup orange juice
2 ripe nectarines, unpeeled, pitted and sliced
1 bunch of watercress, tough ends discarded, coarsely chopped
4 teaspoons red wine vinegar
4 large burrito-size flour tortillas

1. Heat the oil in a large nonstick skillet over medium-high heat. Add the pork and onions and cook, turning frequently, until the pork is firm to the touch and still slightly pink in the center, about 15 to 20 minutes. Season with half the salt and pepper, or to taste, and transfer the pork to a cutting board. Allow to rest for 5 minutes. Add the bourbon and orange juice to the skillet. Simmer until almost all the juices are absorbed and a little sauce remains, about 2 to 3 minutes. Meanwhile, thinly slice the pork. Turn off the heat and return the sliced pork to the pan. Stir to combine.

2. While the pork is cooking, toss the nectarines and watercress in a medium bowl with the vinegar.

3. To assemble: Heat the tortillas, one at a time, directly on a gas flame, on a grill, or in a hot skillet, turning frequently, until hot and pliable, about 5 to 15 seconds each. Or heat, stacked, in the microwave (see page 19). Distribute a quarter of the pork and onions, topped with a quarter of the nectarine salad, in a thick horizontal strip across the bottom third of the tortillas, making sure the ingredients don't quite touch the edges. Fold in the two sides and roll the wrap away from you. Complete the wraps with the remaining ingredients. Or, if you prefer, prepare all at once, assembly-line style.

MAKES 4 WRAPS

Make Ahead/Take Away
The pork and onion mixture may be prepared up to 2 days in advance. When you're ready to eat the wraps, reheat the mixture very gently in the microwave, just until warm, about 1 to 2 minutes. Assemble the wrap with the pork and onion mixture only. Reheat just until warmed through, either sealed in foil in a preheated 350°F oven for 10 to 15 minutes or in the microwave, unsealed, for about 1 minute on high. Open and add the nectarine salad, rewrap, and serve.

Parisian Pocket

 Use your favorite pâté for this lunch. Serve with a salad of the remaining greens, tossed with apple slices and a simple dressing. Each pita can also be cut into 8 triangles for make-ahead appetizers.

4 sandwich-size whole-wheat or white pita pockets, cut in half to make 8 pockets
about 2 teaspoons grainy mustard
8 ounces coarse country or smooth mousse pâté
4 cornichons or gherkins, sliced into quarters lengthwise
12 to 15 watercress sprigs, tough ends removed, or 4 red leaf lettuce leaves, torn into small pieces

To assemble: Open each pita pocket and spread the inside with a 1/4 teaspoon of the mustard. Add an eighth of the pâté, cornichons, and watercress sprigs to each, with the greens peeking out of the top.

MAKES 8 SMALL WRAPS, SERVING 4 AS LUNCH OR 16 TO 30 AS AN APPETIZER

Make Ahead/Take Away
Make up to a day in advance without the greens. Store in the refrigerator, well covered and chilled, to prevent drying. Leave out at room temperature for about 30 minutes, open, add the greens, then serve.

Diner Wrap

 For Americana comfort, try this blue plate special: a mushroom cheeseburger deluxe on smashed potatoes, all in the palm of your hand.

2 medium new potatoes (about 4 ounces each)
½ pound ground beef
½ pound mushrooms, sliced
⅓ cup grated Cheddar cheese or 4 slices of brick cheese
1 8-ounce can tomato sauce
2 teaspoons Worcestershire sauce
¼ teaspoon freshly ground pepper or to taste
2 large burrito-size flour tortillas
1 tablespoon grainy mustard or to taste
2 thin slices of a small onion, optional
8 to 10 slices dill pickle, optional

1. Cover the potatoes with lightly salted water in a small pot. Bring to a boil and boil until fork-tender, 20 to 25 minutes. Leave in the water until ready to use.

2. When the potatoes are almost cooked, preheat a large nonstick skillet over high heat. Form the beef into 1 large patty and add to the pan, searing on one side, about 1 minute. Scatter the mushrooms around the burger and cook, stirring frequently. Turn the burger after 3 to 5 minutes, depending on desired doneness, and continue cooking for 3 to 4 minutes (it will continue cooking with the sauce, so undercook it a bit). Top the burger with cheese. Add the tomato sauce, Worcestershire sauce, and pepper to the mushrooms. Immediately reduce the heat to medium, cover, and cook until the sauce has thickened and the cheese is melted, 2 to 3 minutes.

3. To assemble: Heat the tortillas, one at a time, directly on a gas flame, on a grill, or in a hot skillet, turning frequently, until hot and pliable, about 5 to 15 seconds each. Or heat, stacked, in the microwave (see page 19). Spread each tortilla with 1½ teaspoons mustard or to taste. Layer each with a drained potato (smashed with a fork right onto the tortilla), half the cheeseburger, half the sauce, and, if desired, extra onion and pickle, in a thick horizontal strip across the bottom third of the tortillas, making sure the ingredients don't quite touch the edges. Fold in the two sides and roll the wrap away from you.

MAKES 2 WRAPS

Trim the Fat

To make this a low-fat wrap, use ground low-fat turkey instead of beef and cook as described until well done. Instead of $\frac{1}{3}$ cup cheese, use 3 tablespoons. Then, to compensate for the lost flavor, for half of the mushrooms substitute sliced shiitake caps. This is great!

Shortcuts

Buy presliced mushrooms.

Make Ahead/Take Away

Sealed in wax paper, plastic wrap, or foil and refrigerated, the wraps keep for up to 6 hours. Reheat just until warmed through, either sealed in foil in a pre-heated 350°F oven for 10 to 15 minutes or in the microwave, unsealed, for about 1 minute on high.

Carnegie Deli Wrap

 New York's Carnegie Deli is famous for its fabulous corned beef. I love it piled high, with plenty of coleslaw, on seedy rye with a touch of mustard and a crisp dill pickle on the side. Now that I live in New England, this wrap can be assembled in seconds, and it reminds me of home. Extra perk: Cut it open, and there's a pretty spiral inside.

4 lavash rectangles
2½ tablespoons grainy mustard
1 pound sliced corned beef
1⅓ cups coleslaw (about 6 ounces)
¾ to 1 cup thickly sliced dill pickles

To assemble: With a short end of a lavash facing you, spread about 2 slightly rounded teaspoons of the mustard over the entire lavash. Cover with a quarter of the corned beef, followed by a quarter of the coleslaw and pickles, and roll the wrap away from you. Complete the wraps with the remaining ingredients. Or, if you prefer, prepare all at once, assembly-line style. Cut in half on the bias.
MAKES 4 HEARTY WRAPS

Substitutions
Try pastrami or smoked turkey instead of corned beef. Large burrito-size flour tortillas, heated (see page 19), can be used in place of lavash rectangles.

Make Ahead/Take Away
Sealed in plastic, wax paper, or foil and refrigerated, these wraps keep well for up to 2 days before serving. Serve cold or at room temperature.

Joy Luck Pocket

 Tender filet mignon, sesame mayonnaise, and sprigs of watercress are all stuffed into this decadent little pita pocket.

1½ teaspoons vegetable oil
12 ounces filet mignon, well trimmed, cut into 2 thick rounds
1 garlic clove, finely minced
1 pinch aniseeds, optional
1 tablespoon soy sauce
1½ teaspoons rice wine vinegar
1½ teaspoons sugar
3 tablespoons mayonnaise
½ teaspoon sesame oil
2 scallions, both white and green parts, trimmed and chopped
4 sandwich-size pita pockets, top quarter sliced off
1 small bunch of watercress, tough stems removed

1. Heat the oil in a small skillet over medium-high heat. Add the beef and sear on both sides, cooking to the desired doneness, about 3 to 5 minutes on each side. Transfer to a cutting board to cool for 10 minutes.

2. Immediately remove the skillet from the heat and stir in the garlic, aniseeds, soy sauce, vinegar, and sugar. Whisk in the mayonnaise and sesame oil thoroughly, until it is well combined. After the beef has cooled for about 10 minutes, thinly slice it and toss it into the pan with the sesame mayonnaise and scallions.

3. To assemble: Open the pockets and fill each with a quarter of the sesame beef topped with a quarter of the watercress and push the filling down into the pita. Serve immediately.
MAKES 4 WRAPS

Make Ahead/Take Away
Sesame beef can be prepared up to 1 day ahead and chilled. If you are taking it along, pack the sesame beef, watercress, and pita separately. Assemble the wraps right before eating. Serve cold or at room temperature; this does not reheat well.

Spice-Blackened Steak Gyro with Pickled Onions

 If you're a beef lover, you'll adore this succulent steak gyro packed with plenty of flavor. As with all blackened dishes, turn on your oven fan!

1 small onion, sliced
1½ tablespoons red wine vinegar
1 teaspoon sugar
1 teaspoon ground coriander
1 teaspoon onion powder
½ teaspoon peppercorns, cracked with the bottom of a heavy pot
1 8-ounce strip steak
1 teaspoon vegetable oil, plus oil for brushing pita
½ cup beef stock, preferably reduced-sodium
1½ teaspoons Worcestershire sauce
2 pocketless pitas
4 large escarole leaves, tough spines removed

1. Place the onion in a nonmetal measuring cup. Cover with water and a small microwave-safe plate. Microwave on high until the water is boiling, about 5 minutes (or add the onions to a small pot of water on the stove, bring to a boil, then turn off the heat). Let stand for 5 minutes, then drain. Stir in the vinegar and sugar. Chill in the refrigerator for 20 minutes to 3 hours.

2. Combine the coriander, onion power, and crushed peppercorns on a plate. Press the steak into the spices, turning to coat. Add the oil to a nonstick skillet and heat over medium heat. Sear the steak until it reaches the desired doneness, about 4 to 7 minutes on each side. Trans-fer to a cutting board. (The charred bits on the bottom of the pan add to this dish, but if the pan is burned heavily, it can be wiped out carefully, off the heat, with a triple layer of paper towels.) Add the beef stock and Worcestershire sauce to the pan (carefully, because it can splatter) and cook until it is reduced to a quarter of its original volume, about 2 tablespoons, after 3 to 4 minutes. Thinly slice the steak, return to the sauce, and toss. Remove from heat.

3. To assemble: Brush one side of each pita with a little oil. Heat the pita, one at a time, oiled side down, in a hot skillet until slightly crisp but not brittle, about 1 minute each. Lay each pita on a 12-inch square of foil, crisp side down. Layer half the escarole, sauced steak, and drained pickled onions and 1 teaspoon onion pickle juice in a strip down the center of each pita. Roll the bread and foil together into a cone, using the foil for support and to seal the bottom. Peel the foil down as you eat.

MAKES 2 WRAPS

Make Ahead/Take Away

Prepare the onions as described in step 1 up to 3 days in advance and store in the refrigerator. Once assembled, serve the wraps immediately.

Tangier Lamb Tagine
with Spiced Yogurt

 The tempting aroma of this Moroccan-inspired wrap, spiked with sweet raisins, will lure even plain eaters into the kitchen. Harissa is a hot pepper sauce that can be found in a tube or small can at some supermarkets and all specialty stores.

1 cup plain yogurt
2 tablespoons harissa or thick hot chili sauce such as Szechwan
1 pound ground lamb
1 large onion, chopped
1 tablespoon ground cumin
4 teaspoons finely minced peeled fresh ginger
¼ cup raisins
½ teaspoon salt
½ teaspoon freshly ground pepper
1 cup canned chickpeas, drained and rinsed
4 teaspoons fresh lemon juice
4 large burrito-size flour tortillas
10 to 12 ounces prewashed spinach leaves, stems removed
lemon wedges

1. Combine the yogurt and harissa in a small bowl and reserve.

2. Place the lamb, onion, cumin, ginger, raisins, salt, and pepper in a large skillet over a medium heat. Cook, stirring and breaking up the lamb with a wooden spoon, until the meat is cooked and the onions are soft, 5 to 7 minutes. Add the chickpeas. Using a potato masher, mash at least half of them right in the pan, blending them with the meat. Continue to cook, stirring occasionally, until they are warm, 1 to 2 minutes. Add the lemon juice.

3. To assemble: Heat the tortillas, one at a time, directly on a gas flame, on a grill, or in a hot skillet, turning frequently, until hot and pliable, about 5 to 15 seconds each. Or heat, stacked, in the microwave (see page 19). Spread about 2 tablespoons of the spiced yogurt on a warm tortilla, leaving a 1-inch border. Layer a quarter of the spinach and the lamb mixture and another 2 tablespoons spiced yogurt in a thick horizontal strip across the bottom third of the tortilla, making sure the ingredients don't quite touch the edges. Fold in the two sides and roll the wrap away from you. Complete the wraps with the remaining ingredients. Or, if you prefer, prepare all at once, assembly-line style. Cut in half on the bias.

MAKES 4 WRAPS

Trim the Fat

To make this a low-fat wrap, cut the lamb down to 10 ounces of lean lamb. Add ¼ cup more chickpeas and use ⅓ rather than ¼ cup raisins. Use nonfat yogurt instead of regular. To replace the lost moisture, add an additional 3 tablespoons nonfat yogurt in step 1. This works!

Make Ahead/Take Away

Lamb tagine can be made as described in steps 1 and 2 up to 1 day ahead and chilled. Reheat, covered, in the microwave on high, just until warm, about 1 to 2 minutes. Assemble as described. Serve warm.

Athenian Lamb Gyro with Tzatziki

 This light, fresh-tasting version of street vendors' souvlaki can be made easily at home.

about ½ pound boneless lamb chops, well trimmed
1 tablespoon olive oil, plus extra for brushing pita
1 teaspoon ground cumin
1 garlic clove, minced
¼ cup plain yogurt
1 plum tomato, diced
2 pocketless pitas
salt and freshly ground pepper to taste
fresh lemon juice to taste, optional
1 small Kirby cucumber, cut into 8 spears
8 fresh mint leaves (about 2 sprigs)
lemon wedges, optional

1. Rub the lamb chops in 1½ teaspoons of the olive oil, the cumin, and about half the garlic.

2. Combine the yogurt, tomato, and remaining garlic in a small bowl and set aside.

3. Heat the olive oil in a medium skillet over high heat. When the oil is hot, add the lamb. Sear on both sides until it reaches desired doneness (best not cooked more than medium), about 2 minutes on each side. Transfer to a cutting board and cover loosely with foil.

4. To assemble: Brush one side of each pita with a little olive oil. Wipe out the skillet and heat over medium-high heat. Warm the pitas, one at a time, oiled side down, until slightly crisp but not brittle, about 1 minute. Place each on a 12-inch square of foil, crisp side down. Season the meat with salt and pepper and a squeeze of lemon if desired. Slice thinly. Layer half of the meat, cucumber, mint leaves, and yogurt mixture in a strip up the center of each pita. Roll the bread and the foil together into cones, using the foil as support and to seal the bottom. Serve with lemon wedges if desired. Peel the foil down as you eat.

MAKES 2 WRAPS

Trim the Fat

This is a low-fat wrap if the lamb is trimmed of all visible fat. In addition, eliminate the oil from the marinade in step 1, and don't brush the pita with oil. Cook the chops in a nonstick pan, brushed or sprayed with olive oil. Finally, use non-fat yogurt.

Make Ahead/Take Away
The lamb may be marinated up to 24 hours in advance and then seared as described in step 3. Eat immediately after assembling, served warm.

Just-Like-Mom's Lamb Gyro

 This full-flavored gyro uses Mediterranean ingredients—rosemary, garlic, and lamb—in a luscious dark braise that gives the satisfaction of a long-simmered stew in a quarter of the time. (A very economical dish!)

2 lamb shoulder chops (about ¾ pound)
1 medium new potato (about 4 ounces), cut into 8 spears
1 medium onion, sliced
2 large garlic cloves, sliced
1 14.5-ounce can Italian-style stewed tomatoes
1½ teaspoons fresh rosemary leaves or ½ teaspoon dried
¼ teaspoon salt
⅛ teaspoon freshly ground pepper or more to taste
4 pocketless pitas
olive oil for brushing pita

1. Preheat a large skillet over medium-high heat. Add the chops and potato, shaking the pan frequently to keep them from sticking. Cook until well browned, turning once, about 5 minutes per side.
2. Add the onion and garlic and toss to combine. Continue cooking, stirring occasionally, until the onion is slightly softened, about 5 minutes. Add the tomatoes and their juices, rosemary, salt, and pepper. Bring to a boil, then reduce the heat to medium-low. Cover tightly and cook until the lamb is very tender, about 30 minutes.
3. Pull the lamb out of the skillet. When it is cool enough to handle, remove the meat from the bones and sinew. Shred the meat into bite-sized pieces and return it to the skillet, stirring to combine.

4. Preheat the broiler. Brush one side of each pita with olive oil and broil, oiled side up, until slightly crisp but not brittle, about 1 minute. Place each pita, crisp side down, on a 12-inch square of foil. Divide the lamb mixture equally among the pitas, in a strip down the center. Roll the bread and foil together into cones, using the foil as support and to seal the bottom. Peel the foil down as you eat.
MAKES 4 WRAPS

Make Ahead/Take Away
The lamb mixture can be made up to 2 days in advance and refrigerated. Reheat, covered, in a 350°F oven for about 20 minutes or on high in the microwave until warm, about 2 to 5 minutes. Once the wraps are assembled, serve immediately.

Panini Wrap

 Panini are simple, satisfying Italian sandwiches. Often they are as basic as a slice of mozzarella, ripe tomato, and basil leaf on a small crusty roll; other times they are grilled sandwiches with a few layers of seasonal goodies.

2 pita pockets
8 sun-dried tomatoes packed in oil, drained and finely chopped (about
   1½ tablespoons)
8 to 10 very thin slices of prosciutto, or enough to cover each pita
½ pound fresh mozzarella, chopped or coarsely grated
about 16 fresh basil leaves

1. Preheat the broiler. Carefully split the pita pockets in half with a sharp paring knife so that you have 4 rounds.

2. To assemble: Layer the chopped tomatoes, a thin layer of prosciutto, and the mozzarella evenly over the pita rounds, making sure the ingredients don't quite touch the edges. Broil just until the cheese starts to melt, about 1 minute. Remove from the broiler and top with basil. Immediately roll into wraps. Cut on the bias.

MAKES 4 WRAPS

Make Ahead/Take Away
These can be assembled up to a day in advance, then covered well and stored in the refrigerator. When you are ready to eat, broil, top with basil, wrap, and serve immediately.

10 cheese and egg wraps

Sometimes you can't beat the rich flavor of eggs or warm melted cheese. So this short chapter wraps it up with the occasional egg and/or cheese meal. After all, variety is the spice of life.

You're sure to be driven wild by the contrast of runny cheese inside crusty tortillas in the baked Camembert and Apple Chutney Crisp or the pan-seared Blueberry Nectarine Blintz. (Substitute your favorite cheese or fruit, using the recipe quantities as general guides.) Many of the cheese wraps, like Double-Fig Wrap with Prosciutto and Mascarpone, also make great salad courses or light lunches, served with a handful of tossed greens. Others, like the Quick Chèvre Salad Wrap or the low-fat Cheese-in-a-Snap Wrap, make quick meals on their own.

Eggs make fast wraps too. In 10 minutes the elegant Frittata Flip graces your breakfast table. Or, when nothing's in the house, you can just reach for the egg carton and improvise a speedy cook-and-eat wrap. Flexible eggs will take on any of your favorite flavors, from subtle herbs, like dill, to hot chilies and salsa. I enjoy eggs scrambled with Asian stir-fry flavors like ginger and scallion and the added crunch of water chestnuts. As it turns out, my editor, Katie Workman, wraps up eggs for quick meals too. We both love to dream up egg wraps, using soft scrambled eggs with fresh herbs or spices and vegetables, potatoes, or cheese. For extra zing, we fold them into tortillas spread with household staples like mango chutney, hoisin sauce, or a dash of our favorite hot sauce (mine's Cholula). Use tortillas of any size or shape, but I like corn or small taco-size flour tortillas, although you can also fill pita pockets or even mountain bread. Or, when you have a few extra minutes and you like south-of-the-border flavors, try Taos Breakfast Roll with Ancho Chili Ketchup. The ancho chili ketchup is so tasty, it has replaced standard ketchup in my house.

For a change of pace, keep hard-cooked eggs on hand to make egg salad wraps. I included two, better-than-ever variations on the classic whole-wheat egg salad sandwich, Egg Salad Rémoulade, and a very Provençal Niçoise Egg Salad with Olive Tapenade. Be sure to check cooking directions for the perfect, peelable, hard-cooked egg every time.

CHEESE AND EGG

Blueberry Nectarine Blintz

Camembert and Apple Chutney Crisp

Cheese-in-a-Snap Wrap

Double-Fig Wrap with Prosciutto and Mascarpone

Quick Chèvre Salad Wrap

Egg Salad Rémoulade

Niçoise Egg Salad with Olive Tapenade

Frittata Flip

Taos Breakfast Roll with Ancho Chili Ketchup

Blueberry Nectarine Blintz

 I adore these crisp tortillas filled with sweet ricotta and topped with fresh blueberry sauce. They make a romantic brunch stunning dessert wrap.

1 cup blueberries (½ pint)
3½ tablespoons sugar
1½ teaspoons grated peeled fresh ginger
1 cup whole-milk ricotta cheese at room temperature
1 teaspoon vanilla extract
2 small ripe nectarines, pitted and sliced
2 small taco-size flour tortillas
1 teaspoon unsalted butter
2 tablespoons sliced almonds

1. To make the sauce: Combine the blueberries, 2 tablespoons of the sugar, and ½ teaspoon of the ginger in a small saucepan with 2 tablespoons water. Heat over medium-high heat, stirring frequently, just until some of the berries burst and a sauce forms, adding up to 2 tablespoons extra water if necessary. Remove from the heat and reserve.

2. To make the filling: Mix the ricotta, vanilla, 1 sliced nectarine, remaining 1½ tablespoons sugar, and remaining 1 teaspoon grated ginger.

3. To assemble: Place half the filling in the center of each tortilla. Carefully fold in the sides and roll, tucking in the ends carefully. (If you prefer, you may heat the tortillas to make them more pliable, but if you work carefully, it isn't essential.)

4. To cook: Heat the butter in a large nonstick skillet over medium heat. Carefully add the blintzes and cook, until well browned on both sides and warm all the way through, about 2 to 4 minutes on each side. Add the nuts during the last minute of cooking, stirring frequently to prevent burning.

5. To serve: Place a blintz in the center of each plate. Spoon the blueberry sauce over. Sprinkle with the remaining nectarine slices and the toasted nuts. Serve immediately.

MAKES 2 WRAPS

Trim the Fat

To reduce fat, substitute ¾ cup low-fat ricotta for the cup of whole-milk cheese.

Make Ahead/Take Away

Assemble the blintzes up to 2 hours before cooking and chill. Take them out of the refrigerator 30 minutes before cooking, then proceed with the recipe. Once cooked, serve them immediately.

Camembert and Apple Chutney Crisp

 For a unique cheese course or light meal, cut the recipe in half and serve the crunchy wrap propped up at an angle, nestled in a green salad, topped with toasted almonds or in a walnut dressing. Camembert is a cheese that's widely available in supermarkets and cheese shops.

1 large Golden Delicious apple, cored and cut into ½-inch dice with the skin on
2 tablespoons minced shallots
1 tablespoon raisins
2 teaspoons cider vinegar
½ teaspoon packed brown sugar
½ teaspoon grated peeled fresh ginger
pinch of hot red pepper flakes
4 rounds of mountain bread
5 ounces Camembert at room temperature, cut or torn into 12 pieces or so

1. Preheat the oven to 425°F. In a medium bowl, combine the apple, shallots, raisins, vinegar, brown sugar, ginger, and red pepper flakes. Let sit for 10 minutes.

2. To assemble: Heat the mountain bread, one at a time, directly over a gas flame or grill, or in a hot skillet, turning frequently, just until pliable, about 5 to 15 seconds each. Scatter 3 pieces of cheese in the center of a round of mountain bread. Top with a quarter of the apple chutney. Fold in the two sides and roll. Complete the wraps with the remaining ingredients. Or, if you prefer, prepare them all at once, assembly-line style.

3. To cook: Lightly oil a baking sheet and heat in the oven for 5 minutes. Carefully add the wraps, seam side down, and bake until crisp on one side, then turn and bake until the second side is crisp, about 10 minutes total. Remove from the oven and allow to sit for 5 minutes. Serve hot or warm, cut in half on the bias with a serrated knife.

MAKES 4 WRAPS

Substitutions
Use Brie instead of Camembert.

Make Ahead/Take Away
Assemble up to 3 hours before cooking and hold at room temperature. When ready to cook, proceed with the recipe. Once cooked, serve warm.

Cheese-in-a-Snap Wrap

 If you keep cottage cheese in the house and you're in a rush, these make healthy fast-food wraps. A warm tortilla wrapped around cool cheese is more satisfying than you might imagine, so eat these immediately before the contrast fades.

I. CHEESE SALAD WRAP
1 garlic clove
¼ teaspoon kosher salt
1 tablespoon balsamic vinegar
2 teaspoons olive oil, preferably fruity
2 cups loosely packed mesclun lettuce mix (about 2 ounces)
2 small taco-size flour tortillas
½ cup cottage cheese

1. In a shallow bowl, using a fork, mash the garlic into the salt. Add the vinegar and oil and stir to combine. Let sit for 1 to 5 minutes to infuse the dressing with garlic. Discard the garlic. Add the mesclun to the bowl and toss.

2. To assemble: Heat the tortillas, one at a time, directly on a gas flame, on a grill, or in a hot skillet, turning frequently, until warm and pliable, about 5 to 15 seconds each. Top the bottom third of each tortilla with half of the cottage cheese and salad, with the greens sticking out over the right side. Fold in the left side and then roll up and away from you into a wrap.

II. CHEESE WRAP WITH CRUNCHY SCALLIONS AND HOT SAUCE
2 small taco-size flour tortillas
½ cup cottage cheese

1 small scallion, both white and green parts, trimmed, halved lengthwise, and cut into 2-inch pieces
hot sauce of your choice to taste

To assemble: Heat the tortillas, one at a time directly on a gas flame, on a grill, or in a hot skillet, turning frequently, until warm and pliable, about 5 to 15 seconds each. Top the bottom third of each tortilla with half of the cottage cheese and scallions and hot sauce to taste. Roll the wraps away from you. Serve immediately.

III. CORN-CHEESE TORTILLA WITH SALSA
2 corn tortillas
⅓ cup cottage cheese
3 tablespoons medium salsa
8 to 10 cilantro leaves
2 green or yellow bell pepper spears

To assemble: Wet your hands and rub them across the tortillas. Heat them all at once in a hot skillet, turning them continuously with tongs until they are soft, about 1 minute. Top the bottom third of each tortilla with half the cottage cheese, salsa, and cilantro and a pepper spear sticking out over the right side. Fold in the left side and roll up and away from you into a wrap.

MAKES 2 WRAPS

Substitutions

This is a flexible recipe, so substitute your favorite ingredients or whatever you have in your pantry.

Trim the Fat

Recipe I is a low-fat wrap if you omit the oil. Recipes II and III are low in fat already. If you want to reduce the fat further, use a low-fat cottage cheese.

Make Ahead/Take Away

Serve immediately.

Double-Fig Wrap with Proscuitto and Mascarpone

 A delectable play on the classic Italian combination of figs and prosciutto. Serve for a light lunch, cheese course, or, as I did, on a picnic, accompanied by a salad. Happily, mascarpone, an Italian fresh cheese, is now widely available, often in well-stocked supermarkets. It has an elegant, slightly sweet flavor and smooth texture. What do you do with leftovers? I used mine, beaten with a little sugar and vanilla, as a dip for fresh strawberries.

4 small fajita-size flour tortillas
¼ cup mascarpone cheese
5 ounces prosciutto, preferably imported, thinly sliced
4 dried figs, thinly sliced
4 fresh figs, cut into eighths
**2 teaspoons chopped fresh mint or ½ teaspoon fresh thyme leaves,
   optional**
freshly ground pepper to taste

To assemble: Heat the tortillas, one at a time, directly on a gas flame, on a grill, or in a hot skillet, turning frequently, until hot and pliable, about 5 to 15 seconds each. Or heat, stacked, in the microwave (see page 19). Layer a tortilla with 1 tablespoon mascarpone, topped with a quarter of the prosciutto, figs, and herbs and pepper, in a thick horizontal strip across the bottom third of the tortillas, making sure the ingredients don't quite touch the edges. Fold in the two sides and roll the wrap away from you. Complete the wraps with the remaining ingredients. Or, if you prefer, prepare all at once, assembly-line style. Cut in half on the bias.

MAKES 4 WRAPS

Substitutions
If you can't find mascarpone, use softened cream cheese.

Make Ahead/Take Away
Sealed in plastic wrap, wax paper, or foil and refrigerated, these wraps keep well for up to 8 hours. Take out of the refrigerator 30 minutes before serving. Serve cool or at room temperature.

Quick Chèvre Salad Wrap

 The cream cheese–olive sandwich gets a college education.

3 rounds of whole-wheat or white mountain bread
1 3.5-ounce log of chèvre, plain or herbed
freshly ground pepper to taste
3 large green (Sicilian) olives, pitted and chopped
½ yellow or red bell pepper, sliced into 6 strips
3 scallions, green part only, trimmed and cut in half
12 arugula leaves (1 small bunch)

To assemble: Heat the mountain bread, one round at a time, directly over a gas flame or grill, or in a hot skillet, turning frequently, until warm and pliable, about 15 to 20 seconds each. Lay a piece of mountain bread round on the counter. Spread with a third of the chèvre, making sure it doesn't quite touch the edges. Top with pepper. Press a third of the olives into the cheese, then lay 2 pepper strips, a third of the scallion greens, and 4 arugula leaves across the center so that the greens stick out over the right side. Fold in the left side and roll the wrap away from you. Complete the wraps with the remaining ingredients. Or, if you prefer, prepare all at once, assembly-line style.
MAKES 3 WRAPS

Substitutions
You can use watercress instead of arugula.

Make Ahead/Take Away
Wrapped tightly with both sides folded in, these will keep well, sealed in wax paper, plastic wrap, or foil, for up to 8 hours. Bring to room temperature for the best flavor.

Egg Salad Rémoulade

 Both old-fashioned and better than ever.

3 large eggs
¼ cup mayonnaise
2 teaspoons Dijon mustard
3 rounds of whole-wheat mountain bread
12 spinach leaves
⅔ cup coarsely chopped red onion
3 tablespoons chopped fresh dill
6 cornichons or gherkins, sliced
salt and freshly ground pepper to taste

1. Place 3 eggs in a small pot and cover with 1 inch of cold water. Cook, uncovered, over high heat just until it starts to boil. Remove from the heat, cover the pan, and let sit for 15 minutes. Run the eggs under cold water (or let sit in a bowl of ice-cold water, changing the water as needed, until well chilled). Peel and slice.
2. Mix the mayonnaise and mustard in a medium bowl.
3. To assemble: Heat the mountain bread rounds, one at a time, in a hot skillet, turning frequently, until warm and pliable, about 5 to 15 seconds each. Lay each round on top of a sheet of wax paper. Spread each with about 1 tablespoon of the mustard-mayonnaise mixture. Add the egg to the remaining mustard-mayonnaise in the bowl and mix. Layer each round with 4 spinach leaves, spread out evenly, a third of the egg mixture, red onion, dill, and cornichons, and salt and pepper, in a thick horizontal strip across the bottom third of the tortillas, making sure the ingredients don't quite touch the edges. Roll the wrap away from you (don't fold in the sides), being careful not to include the wax paper in the spiral. Cut in half on the bias. Peel the wax paper down as you eat.
MAKES 3 WRAPS

Make Ahead/Take Away
Sealed in plastic wrap, wax paper, or foil and refrigerated, these wraps keep well for up to 4 hours. Serve cold or at room temperature.

Niçoise Egg Salad with Olive Tapenade

 Take these wraps along, icy cold, for a summer lunch or picnic.

4 large eggs
1 small tomato, chopped
1 celery rib, diced
2 tablespoons chopped celery leaves
½ cup chopped Vidalia, Spanish, or red onion
15 wrinkled, oil-cured or 18 Kalamata olives, pitted
1 tablespoon drained capers
1 teaspoon anchovy paste
⅛ teaspoon freshly ground pepper
2 teaspoons olive oil, preferably fruity
1½ tablespoons fresh lemon juice
4 large burrito-size flour tortillas

1. Place 3 eggs in a small pot and cover with cold water. Cook over high heat just until it starts to boil. Remove from the heat, cover the pan, and let sit for 15 minutes. Let the eggs sit in a bowl of ice water until well chilled. Peel and chop. Combine in a small bowl with the tomato, celery, and onion. Set aside.

2. In a food processor, pulse the olives, capers, anchovy paste, and pepper until coarsely chopped. Add the olive oil and lemon juice and pulse to combine.

3. To assemble: Heat the tortillas, one at a time, directly on a gas flame, on a grill, or in a hot skillet, turning frequently, until hot and pliable, about 5 to 15 seconds each. Or heat, stacked, in the microwave (see page 19). Lay a tortilla on a sheet of wax paper. Spread with 1 tablespoon of tapenade. Distribute a quarter of the egg mixture, drizzled with some of the tapenade, in a thick horizontal strip across the bottom third of each tortilla, making sure the ingredients don't quite touch the edges. Fold in the two sides and roll the wrap away from you, being careful not to include the wax paper in the spiral. Complete the wraps with the remaining ingredients. Or, if you prefer, prepare all at once, assembly-line style. Cut in half on the bias.

MAKES 4 WRAPS

Make Ahead/Take Away
The tapenade and eggs can both be prepared a day in advance and chilled. Sealed in plastic wrap, wax paper, or foil and refrigerated, these wraps will keep well for up to 6 hours before serving. Serve at room temperature or cold.

Frittata Flip

 Wondering what to do with the salmon left over from Sunday brunch? Wrap it up! Italy meets Scandinavia in this thin frittata with smoked salmon and dill-mustard sauce. Serve for breakfast or brunch with a glass of freshly squeezed juice or some fruit salad or for dinner with a simple salad.

12 sugar snap peas, tough strings removed
1 tablespoon grainy mustard
1½ teaspoons honey
1 teaspoon packed chopped fresh dill
2 large eggs
1 tablespoon chopped fresh chives
freshly ground pepper to taste
1 teaspoon unsalted butter
2 small fajita-size flour tortillas
1½ ounces smoked salmon (3 to 4 slices)
1 ripe plum tomato, chopped

1. Bring a small pot of water to a boil. Add the sugar snaps and cook for 1 minute. Drain and run under cold water. Set aside. Combine the mustard, honey, and dill in a small bowl and set aside.

2. Whisk together the eggs, chives, and pepper in a small bowl. Heat the butter in a medium nonstick pan over medium heat. Add the eggs and cook, without stirring, until they are just set into a thin frittata and the top is set, about 2 minutes.

3. To assemble: Heat the tortillas, one at a time, directly on a gas flame, on a grill, or in a hot skillet, turning frequently, until hot and pliable, about 5 to 15 seconds each. Or heat, stacked, in the microwave (see page 19). Divide the fritatta in half across the middle and add half to each tortilla, lining the rounded edge of each fritatta half with the bottom edge of each tortilla. Top the frittata with a layer of the mustard-honey-dill mixture, followed by half of the salmon, snap peas, and plum tomatoes. Roll away from you into a wrap. Cut in half on the bias with a very sharp or serrated knife.

MAKES 2 WRAPS

Substitutions

If sugar snaps are not available, substitute asparagus or green beans. In step 1, cook 3 to 4 asparagus, tough ends removed, cut into 1½- to 2-inch pieces, or 5 or 6 green beans, trimmed and halved, until tender-crisp, about 5 minutes. Substitute parsley or cilantro for the dill.

Make Ahead/Take Away

These are best served warm, but also good at room temperature. Sealed in plastic wrap, wax paper, or foil and refrigerated, these wraps will keep well for up to 3 hours. Take them out of the refrigerator 30 minutes before serving.

Taos Breakfast Roll
with Ancho Chili Ketchup

 Fried eggs and oniony hash browns with a spicy homemade ketchup that leaves the bottled stuff in the dust. The ketchup takes a little effort to prepare, but is well worth it. (You'll have a little left over, but it will keep for 2 weeks and is also terrific with grilled steak or chicken.) Ancho chili peppers are dried poblanos; they have a distinctive deep flavor. You can find them in most supermarkets and all specialty food stores.

1 large waxy boiling potato, scrubbed and grated
1 medium onion, cut in half, half grated and half left whole
salt to taste
1 dried ancho chili (3 to 4 inches)
1 10-ounce can diced tomatoes and green chilies, drained
1 tablespoon red wine vinegar or to taste
2 teaspoons sugar or to taste
2 teaspoons vegetable oil
2 large eggs
2 large burrito-size flour tortillas
¼ cup grated Cheddar cheese, optional
1 tablespoon chopped cilantro, optional

1. Toss together the potato, grated onion, and ½ teaspoon salt and allow to drain in a colander for 15 minutes.

2. To make the ketchup: Toast the ancho chili pepper with the whole onion half in a large dry nonstick skillet over medium heat until the ancho is dark but not black and the onion is lightly browned, about 2 minutes on each side (reserve the pan). Add the onion half to a blender and reserve. Bring water to a boil in a small saucepan. Drop in the chili and reduce the heat to a very low simmer until the chili is soft, about 3 minutes. Drain. Remove the stem and seeds and place in the food processor with the onion half. Add the drained tomatoes and chilies. Blend until smooth.

3. Return the blended ketchup to the saucepan and simmer over low heat for 5 to 10 minutes. Remove from the heat and season with vinegar and sugar. (The flavor of anchos tends to differ. You are looking for a deep flavor that is slightly spicy and a tad sweet and sour.)

4. Squeeze out any remaining liquid from the potatoes, by hand or in a kitchen towel. Heat the oil in the reserved non-stick skillet over medium-high heat. Add the potatoes and onion. Cook, stirring frequently, until golden brown, about 10 minutes. Push aside the potatoes in the pan to allow room for the eggs. Break the eggs into the skillet and fry until the whites are almost set, then flip the eggs with a spatula, being careful not to break yolks. If you are using them, sprinkle the cheese and cilantro over the eggs and potato. Remove from the heat.

5. To assemble: Heat the tortillas, one at a time, directly on a gas flame, on a grill, or in a hot skillet, turning frequently, until hot and pliable, about 5 to 15 seconds each. Or heat, stacked, in the microwave (see page 19). Spread each tortilla with 2 tablespoons of the ancho chili ketchup, leaving a 1-inch border. Layer with half of the eggs, potatoes, and salt in a thick horizontal strip across the bottom third of the tortillas, making sure the ingredients don't quite touch the edges. Fold in the two sides and roll the wrap away from you. Serve with some of the extra ketchup on the side.

MAKES 2 WRAPS

Shortcuts

Don't toast the chili or onion, and use a quarter, instead of half, of the onion in the ketchup.

Make Ahead/Take Away

Make the ketchup up to 2 weeks in advance. Before using, bring it to room temperature. Once the wraps are assembled, serve them immediately.

index

Conversion Chart
Equivalent Imperial and Metric Measurements

American cooks use standard containers, the 8-ounce cup and a tablespoon that takes exactly 16 level fillings to fill that cup level. Measuring by cup makes it very difficult to give weight equivalents, as a cup of densely packed butter will weigh considerably more than a cup of flour. The easiest way therefore to deal with cup measurements in recipes is to take the amount by volume rather than by weight. Thus the equation reads:

1 cup = 240 ml = 8 fl. oz.   ½ cup = 120 ml = 4 fl. oz.

It is possible to buy a set of American cup measures in major stores around the world.

In the States, butter is often measured in sticks. One stick is the equivalent of 8 tablespoons. One tablespoon of butter is therefore the equivalent to ½ ounce/15 grams.

Liquid Measures

Fluid Ounces	U.S.	Imperial	Milliliters	
	1 teaspoon	1 teaspoon	5	
¼	2 teaspoons	1 dessertspoon	10	
½	1 tablespoon	1 tablespoon	14	
1	2 tablespoons	2 tablespoons	28	
2	¼ cup	4 tablespoons	56	
4	½ cup		110	
5		¼ pint or 1 gill	140	
6	¾ cup		170	
8	1 cup		225	
9			250,	¼ liter
10	1¼ cups	½ pint	280	
12	1½ cups		340	
15		¾ pint	420	
16	2 cups		450	
18	2¼ cups		500,	½ liter
20	2½ cups	1 pint	560	
24	3 cups		675	
25		1¼ pints	700	
27	3½ cups		750	
30	3¾ cups	1½ pints	840	
32	4 cups or 1 quart		900	
35		1¾ pints	980	
36	4½ cups		1000,	1 liter
40	5 cups	2 pints or 1 quart	1120	

Solid Measures

U.S. and Imperial Measures		Metric Measures	
Ounces	Pounds	Grams	Kilos
1		28	
2		56	
3½		100	
4	¼	112	
5		140	
6		168	
8	½	225	
9		250	¼
12	¾	340	
16	1	450	
18		500	½
20	1¼	560	
24	1½	675	
27		750	¾
28	1¾	780	
32	2	900	
36	2¼	1000	1
40	2½	1100	
48	3	1350	
54		1500	1½

Oven Temperature Equivalents

Fahrenheit	Celsius	Gas Mark	Description
225	110	¼	Cool
250	130	½	
275	140	1	Very Slow
300	150	2	
325	170	3	Slow
350	180	4	Moderate
375	190	5	
400	200	6	Moderately Hot
425	220	7	Fairly Hot
450	230	8	Hot
475	240	9	Very Hot
500	250	10	Extremely Hot

Any broiling recipes can be used with the grill of the oven, but beware of high-temperature grills.

Equivalents for Ingredients

arugala—rocket
beet—beetroot
coarse salt—kitchen salt

eggplant—aubergine
lima beans—broad beans
scallion—spring onion

snowpeas—mangetout
squash—courgettes or marrow
zucchini—courgettes or marrow